Urban Renewal Administration

Urban Renewal Administration

practices, procedures, record keeping

BY EMANUEL GORLAND

Wayne State University Press, Detroit, 1971

Contents

* Appendices 2, 3, 6, 7, 8 and 9 are in a separate envelope inside the slipcase.

Acknowledgments

The preparation of this book spanned a period of several years during which time the United States Department of Housing and Urban Development was completely reorganized, its required practices and procedures drastically changed, and its *Urban Renewal Manual* replaced by the *Urban Renewal Handbook*. This state of flux made the job difficult and at times very discouraging. This book was completed only through the assistance and encouragement of many persons. Grateful acknowledgment is expressed to Ralph Herod, Acting Assistant Secretary for Renewal and Housing Management, Department of Housing and Urban Development, his assistant, Robert C. Scalia, and their staff at Central Office, Washington, D. C., and Thomas J. Kilbride, Assistant Regional Administrator, and his staff at the Region IV Offices in Chicago, for reviewing the manuscript and making constructive suggestions; E. Earl Newkirk, Associate Director for Renewal, National Association of Housing and Redevelopment Officials, and Mark K. Herley, Assistant Director, Detroit Housing Commission, for their encouragement and constructive suggestions; Richard Fosmoen, Urban Renewal Director, City of Ferndale, Michigan, for his recommendations concerning the suggested filing system.

The entire staff of the Office of Community Improvement, Lincoln Park, Michigan, for its help, and special appreciation to Troy Alley for his recommendations concerning property acquisition and disposition; Cleda Cofer for her recommendations concerning budgets, reports, and financing; Darlene Spence for her recommendations concerning accounting, and tax credits and rebates.

Max F. Schiebold, President of the Lincoln Park City Council and liaison councilman to the Office of Community Improvement for his interest, encouragement, and recommendations from the point of view of a knowledgeable elected public official.

Foremost, words cannot express my deep appreciation to my wife Gertrude for her confidence, encouragement, and cheerful sacrifice of countless evenings and weekends of recreation while I labored on this book.

11

Preface

The purpose of this book is six-fold. It will provide:
 1. A primer to assist the urban renewal administrator in establishing sound administrative practices and procedures.
 2. A guide in the establishment of a well organized system of record keeping to assist various staff personnel in carrying out their assigned tasks.
 3. Basic information for city managers, mayors, commissioners, councilmen, and other public officials on how to establish a renewal program, how to select planners and a director, and how to collect pertinent information which will assist in evaluating the administration of a program.
 4. A means to acquaint staff personnel with aspects of the program to which they are not normally exposed, thus forming the basis of more positive and constructive interrelationships between agency employees.
 5. Project planners and various other consultants with a broader understanding of project execution activities to help in formulating more realistic plans and proposals.
 6. A text book for the teaching of urban renewal.

It is not the purpose of this book to go into procedural details or specific requirements of the United States Department of Housing and Urban Development (HUD). Those details and requirements are contained in the *Urban Renewal Handbook*, the *Neighborhood Development Program Handbook*, and various other directives issued by HUD.

This book is planned to be used with the handbooks for quick reference. Those numbers adjacent to division and subdivision titles and in the text, for example, 7218.1, refer to the applicable section of the handbooks. Sections 7200 through 7228 are located in the *Urban Renewal Handbook*. Sections 7380 through 7389 are located in the *Neighborhood Development Program Handbook*. The number of the *Workable Program for Community Improvement Handbook* is 7100.1.

The first time the names of the various departments and agencies of government or commonly used terms are mentioned in the text, the full form is used with its abbreviation in parentheses following. Thereafter, only the abbreviation is used. An inclusive list of abbreviations is on page 145.

chapter 1

Introduction

WHAT IS URBAN RENEWAL?

Urban renewal is a term used to describe a process in which communities improve themselves by eliminating slums and other substandard areas, checking blight, redesigning poorly planned or outmoded physical patterns, providing choice land for new development, and where feasible, conserving and upgrading salvable property and areas. Many communities have undertaken urban renewal activities, generally on a limited scale, without federal financial help, but as federal financial assistance has been the major incentive toward community renewal in the great majority of cities in the United States in the past two decades, the term *urban renewal* has become almost synonymous with the federally assisted program. Urban renewal, however, may be privately financed and carried out through developments such as Rockefeller Center in New York City and the Golden Triangle in Pittsburgh. The practices and procedures outlined in this book are oriented toward the federally assisted program.

Blight is a disease manifested by poor housing and living environment, substandard buildings, and a high ratio of social and economic ills. Blighted areas generally yield low tax revenue in contrast with the cost of public services required for such areas, such as welfare, police and fire protection, public health and sanitation. Blight is contagious. It spreads rapidly, impairing human and property values in its wake.

Urban renewal programs are locally initiated, planned, and administered within the guidelines established by Congress and the Department of Housing and Urban Development (HUD). In effect they constitute a working partnership between the local and federal governments which results in the elimination of blight and deterioration; the improvement of the living and housing environment of the people; the rejuvenation and revitalization of the community's business core; the improvement of the urban pattern through the development of more compatible land uses for new housing, commerce, industry, off-street parking, schools, parks, and other public facilities. Urban renewal programs broaden the economic base of the community and stimulate the pride and positive human values of its citzens.

RED TAPE

Since the inception of the federally assisted urban renewal program, the maze of red tape involved in its administration has grown to monumental proportions on both the local and federal levels. Local administrators have felt that in many cases regulations were arbitrarily required by HUD solely for the sake of regulation or as a means of empire building among minor HUD officials who were assigned to review submitted documentation and direct the resulting paper shuffling.

Prior to 1969, efforts and suggestions aimed at cutting red tape seemed to fall on deaf ears. In 1969 Lawrence M. Cox, a former local administrator (Norfolk, Virginia), was appointed as HUD assistant secretary for Renewal and Housing Management. Both Secretary Cox, and his Acting Deputy Assistant Secretary for Renewal Management Ralph Herod, another former local administrator (Sacramento, California, and St. Louis, Missouri), were fully cognizant of the problem.

Shortly after assuming his position, Assistant Secretary Cox requested that the National Association of Housing and Redevelopment Officials (NAHRO) review and analyze HUD urban renewal regulations and requirements to determine specific methods of decentralizing responsibility and simplifying procedures.

Among the study suggestions made by Assistant Secretary Cox were:
1. Elimination of unnecessary processing requirements.
2. Acceleration of the renewal process.
3. Reduction of administrative support activities to an absolute minimum.
4. Identification of those areas where responsible local judgment can be substituted for prior federal reviews and approvals.
5. Identification of ways to increase the sense of local responsibility,

particularly that of the boards of the Local Public Agency (LPA) and local governing bodies.

6. Consideration of possible use of local certifications (with sanctions against misrepresentation) in lieu of HUD requirements for review and approval prior to specific action.

Recommendations to Reduce Red Tape

In compliance with the request of Assistant Secretary Cox, the NAHRO Working Committee on Renewal submitted a report containing a long list of recommendations. It advised that some of the recommendations could be implemented on an immediate basis, while others would require substantial revision of existing regulations. Other recommendations would require new legislation.

The report stated:

> The major recommendation of the Working Group is to make maximum use of a "proclaimer procedure" whereby governing bodies of LPA's (or localities, where appropriate) would certify to the fact that program activities are in accord with Federal and local statutes and regulations. Such certification would be in lieu of the submission of detailed documentation to HUD for their approval. Where we have recommended the use of a "proclaimer," we recognize that it carries with it a requirement for responsible local action. We recommend that the appropriate proclaimer developed for each case contain a statement of the steps taken and facts considered by the LPA in coming to their decision. We recognize that any misrepresentation of facts made under the "proclaimer" concept would be subject to appropriate sanctions applicable to the specific action. In turn, it would be expected that HUD would accept all such proclaimers subject only to sample post-audits.

In addition to the request to NAHRO, HUD regional administrators were directed to meet with representatives of state urban renewal associations and other knowledgeable local administrators for their recommendations concerning ways and means of cutting the red tape. The feedback from these recommendations was forwarded from the regional offices to the central office of HUD in Washington, D.C.

What Is the Proclaimer Concept?

In an address to the National Conference of NAHRO held at Bal Harbour, Florida, on October 13, 1969, Assistant Secretary Cox in explaining the proclaimer policy stated:

> Basically, it is a technique designed to reverse HUD's long-standing operating policy, which seems based on the assumption that all local officials are either

incompetent or crooked, or both, and should be judged guilty until proven innocent.

Operating on that assumption, the Department has developed a web of regulations and procedures which require a review or inspection and prior approval of every conceivable matter where trouble might arise.

The result has been a steady erosion of the locality's sense of responsibility, since everyone assumes that HUD will tell the locality what it must do anyway. It has also led to the stifling of local imagination and innovation at the very time when it is needed most.

The proclaimer concept, in contrast, is based on a principle of trust. It is a technique for giving the city the responsibility and flexibility, as well as the accountability it should have for its actions.

The proclaimer itself is a duly signed certification that will substitute for the documentation now submitted for prior review and approval by HUD. This proclaimer will serve as a certification by responsible local officials of the facts and information recited in the document. The proclaimer will be accepted by us without further review or approval, though it will be subject to post-audit as deemed necessary.

This means the locality will be able to proceed as fast as its capabilities permit, it will no longer be held up for interminable lengths of time while HUD reviews a document, sends it back for further information or change, then re-examines the resubmitted material, thus creating the back-and-forth, stop-and-go situation you know so well.

This does not mean that proclaimers will substitute for all submissions and reviews now required. But it will apply to as many as it can, consistent with proper protection of the public interest.

We intend to make the adoption or enactment of a proclaimer a significant action on the part of the local community.

The recitation of the facts and circumstances contained in the proclaimer will serve as a point-by-point reminder of the obligations and responsibilities which the community has freely chosen to accept, after careful consideration and deliberate judgment.

The proclaimer will be signed by the appropriate local official or officials, depending on the nature of the matter at hand. It may be a professional, such as the engineer or architect, or the executive director, the chairman of the local agency, the mayor, or any combination of them, depending on the nature of the proclaimer.

And the signators will be held accountable for the representations contained in the proclaimer.

We believe this kind of approach, in addition to placing responsibility and accountability where it belongs, will have two other important advantages: (1) it will significantly reduce processing delays in the renewal and housing programs, and (2) it will free up limited staff resources within HUD to begin providing the kind of positive, helpful technical assistance and advice that we should be giving to help our cities get on with the job that needs to be done. And it will make the help available when it is needed, not after the fact.

HUD has already implemented the proclaimer procedure relative to several applications and is studying the potential of further utilization of this procedure.

ADMINISTRATION OF AN URBAN RENEWAL PROGRAM

The administration of an urban renewal program involves many disciplines and extensive contacts with a wide range of government agencies, business firms, organizations, and individuals. Good public and governmental relations are basic ingredients of a successful program.

The establishment of a well organized system of administrative practices, procedures, and record keeping will assist in the proper execution of an urban renewal program through the elimination or reduction of time loss, confusion, and duplication of efforts, and will assist in the proper orientation of personnel charged with the various responsibilities.

The recommendations contained herein are of a general nature. Various projects differ in type and objectives and are subject to variation and adaptation in accordance with diverse local conditions. The size and type of the project or program and the abilities of the various persons employed may determine the scope of individual responsibility. For example, in a small community with a small staff, a single person may be charged with all responsibility concerning several project activities, such as relocation and property management, and may possibly assist in such related activities as property acquisition. In a community with a much larger program there may be specialists assigned to a particular phase of a project activity.

There is a general scarcity of skilled and experienced personnel required to carry out the diverse activities of an urban renewal program. This is often an acute problem for small or medium sized communities or for a community when it is entering into the early stages of its first project. In these cases it is generally the responsibility of the urban renewal director not only to organize and administer the program but to evaluate the abilities of various persons available, delegate responsibility accordingly, and assist in training the persons selected.

There is potential overlapping of responsibilities in a smaller community and so no recommendations are contained herein concerning the person or persons who should be charged with the responsibility of keeping and maintaining the various files and records. Whoever is assigned to these functions, it is still the responsibility of the urban renewal director to assure himself from time to time that the files and other records are properly organized and maintained on a current basis (see Appendix 1: Suggested Filing System).

As record keeping is an integral part of good business procedures, procedural tips and comments are generally kept together with recommendations concerning record keeping. These, in turn, will be discussed under one of the major urban renewal activity classifications that are generally inherent in most projects.

The utilization of proclaimer procedures will not change the basic concepts of good urban renewal project administration but will in many instances facilitate such administration.

chapter 2

How to Organize for Renewal

When the Housing Act of 1949 was enacted by Congress, it provided the basic authorization and framework for federally assisted urban renewal. Subsequent amendments have greatly broadened the original concept. The Housing Act of 1949 was a landmark in that it was tangible recognition by Congress that blight and deterioration in our cities had reached such monumental proportions that the economic capabilities of the cities were generally unable to cope with them. It also provided financial assistance in the form of loans and grants to eligible communities.

After the passage of the Housing Act, most states ultimately enacted the necessary enabling legislation granting local communities the opportunity to utilize the financial assistance provided by Congress. Within the framework of its state legislation, communities throughout the country passed the necessary resolutions or ordinances establishing the LPA, and designating and defining its powers in carrying out a local urban renewal program.

In the early years, the complexities of the urban renewal process and procedures were beyond the ability of a vast number of local officials to comprehend. The federal requirement that a community adopt a Workable Program for Community Improvement, which included comprehensive planning, appeared to put additional roadblocks in the federal funds being offered. The need of the community for expert advice in initiating a program and preparing the necessary applications, in addition to carrying out the necessary project and community planning activities, resulted in a rapid growth and expansion of planning consultant firms. These firms were a substantial factor in the wide acceptance of urban renewal. Many persons originally involved in project planning later became project administrators.

Unfortunately, the demand for qualified planners far outstripped the supply. Many of the firms were forced to hire inexperienced persons. This factor, coupled with the planner's general lack of knowledge concerning project execution problems, often led to some sad experiences on the part of the local community, such as long delays in processing defective applications, delays in starting project execution activities, loss of non-cash credits, and the necessity for subsequent amendments of HUD approved applications and contracts resulting therefrom.

SELECTION OF PLANNERS

The shortage of qualified planners is still a critical problem. The community, therefore, should take a close look at the experience and qualifications of a consulting firm before engaging it. The community should not only obtain a list of cities that the firm has served but should also determine the nature of the services performed, the length of time the firm served the city, and whether the firm was reengaged for subsequent projects. It is desirable that some of the cities served by the consultant be contacted to determine their satisfaction.

The community, before entering into a contract with a consulting firm, should ask the firm to submit a list of the particular individuals who, it is anticipated, will work on the job, together with a résumé of their experience and qualifications.

Information concerning the selection of planning consultants is included in this chapter because such consultants very often stimulate local officials to consider an urban renewal program, prior to the establishment of the LPA. Communities both large and small have utilized the services of planning consultants.

The Federal Government, however, will not make any financial contribution toward the cost of establishing the LPA, the preparation of a Workable Program for Community Improvement, or the preparation of many applications for projects or programs. The cost of project planning services will be shared by the Federal Government, provided it is within the amount of the approved budget submitted with the application.

These factors concerning the sharing and non-sharing of costs should be clearly understood by local officials contemplating early contracting with planning or other consultants. It is better not to contract for services required during the project planning or execution stages until approval of the application, or a letter authorizing the incurring of costs, is received from HUD.

The community should also consider the capabilities of its own planning staff, if any, or the services which may be performed by the staff of regional, county, or other agency which may be available to the locality, before contracting with consultants.

ESTABLISHING THE LOCAL PUBLIC AGENCY

Local personnel, including the city attorney, would normally be able to obtain the necessary information relative to the establishment of the LPA. The nature and powers of the LPA differ in the various states. Some provide that the city itself act as the LPA; others provide for the establishment of a redevelopment authority or redevelopment commission; others require that existing housing commissions or authorities act as the LPA for renewal while some states permit the local governing body the right to determine the structure of the LPA.

In order to be eligible for federal financial assistance in urban renewal, it is important that the LPA be properly established. Data concerning local enabling legislation may be obtained in several ways:

1. Request copies of the local legislation adopted by other cities in the same state which are already engaged in urban renewal activities. Most urban renewal directors would gladly assist other communities in initiating a program and in explaining the various aspects to local officials and citizen groups.

2. Contact the HUD regional or area office having jurisdiction over the particular state. The office will, when requested, usually send a representative to the local community to explain the program and give other limited assistance.

3. Contact the National Association of Housing and Redevelopment Officials (NAHRO), The Watergate Building, 2600 Virginia Avenue, N.W., Washington, D.C. 20037, or a nearby NAHRO chapter, or a state association of renewal officials, if one exists in that particular state.

4. Planning consultant firms will generally provide relevant information.

5. Departments of urban affairs under various departmental titles have been established in many states. These departments will generally provide advisory services to the local communities.

If alternative methods of structuring the LPA are permitted by state law, they should be discussed with the city manager and/or the mayor and council and a determination made thereof. The city attorney would then draft the necessary resolution or ordinance for adoption by the local governing body. If the LPA is organized in the form of a commission or an authority, it would come into being upon the appointment and qualification of the commissioners or authority members following the adoption of the necessary enabling legislation by the local legislative body.

WORKABLE PROGRAM

7204.1

The next step in acquiring federal assistance in urban renewal is to obtain HUD certification of the locality's Workable Program for Community Improvement. HUD will not even accept an application for processing if the community does not have a certified Workable Program, unless (1) the locality has requested certification or recertification of same, (2) documentation supporting the request has been submitted to the regional office, and (3) the Workable Program submission has been accepted for processing.

In effect, the Workable Program is a self-analysis by the local community, with regard to certain basic elements, and a projection of the things it proposes to do in future years in meeting established federal criteria. The elements include Codes and Code Enforcement, Planning, Programming and Budgeting, Housing and Relocation, and Citizen Involvement.

Information on the scope, content, and submission of a Workable Program can be obtained from HUD regional or area offices.

DETERMINING THE TYPE OF RENEWAL PROGRAM

General Neighborhood Renewal Program

Comprehensive community planning and various studies made in relation thereto should effectively pinpoint the extent of blight and deterioration in a community. If the area selected for renewal action involves a large contiguous section of the community, it might be desirable to apply for federal assistance in preparing a General Neighborhood Renewal Program (GNRP). The GNRP is a preliminary plan which outlines the urban renewal activities proposed for the General Neighborhood Renewal Area (GNRA), provides a framework for the preparation of urban renewal plans, and indicates generally the land uses, population density, building coverage, prospective requirements for rehabilitation and improvement of property, and any portions of the area contemplated for clearance and redevelopment (see *Urban Renewal Handbook* 7224.1). The GNRP will also recommend the phasing of the urban renewal projects located within its boundaries.

If the area proposed for renewal action appears to be of such a size and scope that the LPA could carry out project activities within a reasonable time, then a GNRP may not be necessary. Elimination of GNRP preparation and approval will speed up the actual renewal process.

National Goals

The shortage of federal funds for urban renewal and the steadily increasing number of communities applying for new projects have created a drain upon available funds. As a result, HUD has established a policy of National Goals and Urban Renewal Priorities in order to obtain maximum utilization of available capital grant funds (see *Urban Renewal Handbook* 7202.1, chap. 1, sec. 1). HUD also provides for certain exemptions from the National Goals.

Conventional Project

In a conventional project, activities are carried out in two separate and distinct stages: 1) Survey and Planning, 2) Project Execution.

Generally during the survey and planning stage, only those activities may be undertaken which are necessary for preparing the prescribed documentation required for a Loan and Grant application to HUD, including the preparation of the Urban Renewal Plan. Under certain conditions and with special HUD approval, the LPA may undertake some other activities during this stage.

Upon the approval of a conventional project by HUD and the execution of a Survey and Planning Contract, grant funds are reserved by HUD to cover the entire commitment of the Federal Government to the project from planning through project completion. A commitment is also made by the Federal Government to provide the LPA with the funds required for the survey and planning stage, on a loan basis.

Following approval of the Loan and Grant application by the local governing body after the required public hearing, and approval by HUD, the project execution stage begins. During this stage, all other project activities are carried out including real estate acquisition, property management, relocation, demolition and site clearance, the construction of project improvements, rehabilitation, and the sale of project land.

Neighborhood Development Program

The adoption of the Neighborhood Development Program (NDP) concept in the Housing and Urban Development Act of 1968 authorized the carrying out of both survey and planning and project execution activities simultaneously. The basic objectives of the NDP were to:

1. Accelerate rehabilitation and development activities with resulting early visible improvements, concurrent with planning activities.
2. Provide a more rapid and flexible response to public and private development opportunities and citizens' needs within critical areas.
3. Prevent the tie-up of vast sums of federal money for long terms of entire project periods, by providing money on an annual cash need basis, thus allowing a spread of funds on a much wider scale.

Benefits and Liabilities of Respective Programs

Although the NDP appears to offer a local community the opportunity for quick action and rapid visible results, it also requires much more precise timing of project activities. Certain activities, such as relocation of site occupants, may be difficult to complete by a timetable. This delays other activities planned in the action year, such as demolition and the construction of public improvements or facilities contemplated as a local non-cash grant-in-aid for the action year. The community would then be required to provide its share of the project costs in cash.

There has been a shortage of federal funds in relation to the demand. A tremendous backlog of pending applications for new projects, the need of financial amendatories to existing contracts due to inflationary factors, and new legislation broadening the cash benefits of the program to affected persons, have created great demands upon the available funds. As a result, many LPAs believe that it is more prudent to undertake a conventional project with the certain reservation of funds for the entire project period than face the uncertainty as to whether funds will be available each year under the NDP.

In any event the local community should analyze the benefits and liabilities of the respective programs in the light of the nature of the project, its needs, and the capabilities of its staff, before determining under which method it should proceed.

chapter 3

How Project Costs Are Shared

7215.1, chap. 1, sec. 1

7385.1, chap. 2, sec. 1

Public officials considering an urban renewal program are first concerned to what extent the Federal Government shares with the municipality the cost of the project. The share of the cost by the Federal Government, or the amount which it contributes to the project, is known as a project capital grant. In order to estimate the amount of a project capital grant, the gross and net project costs will first have to be estimated.

CALCULATING GROSS AND NET PROJECT COSTS

The gross project cost is determined by adding the following:
1. The cost of planning the project (if project is not on a three-fourths capital grant basis with limited costs — explained below).
2. All eligible costs during the project execution period that are paid or payable in cash (item 1 of gross project costs-project expenditures). These costs, payable in accordance with an approved project budget, are fully identified in 7218.1, chap. 2, sec. 1.
3. Cost of non-cash local grants-in-aid (item 2 of gross project cost). These are non-federal expenditures for supporting facilities such as new schools, or project improvements such as sewers, streets, sidewalks, etc., which serve and benefit the project area. These costs are fully identified in 7216.1, chap. 2, sec. 1 (also see chapter 13).

In order to determine the net project cost, obtain the sum of the above items (gross project cost) and subtract therefrom the money that is esti-

28

mated to be realized from the sale of land. This is known as the net project cost.

The amount of the capital grant obtainable from the Federal Government may then be determined as follows:

Two-thirds Grant Basis

A project capital grant for a municipality of over 50,000 population is generally based on two-thirds of the net project cost unless otherwise shown below.

EXAMPLE OF 2/3 GRANT BASIS

Gross project cost	$2,000,000
(Less) Receipts from sale of land	800,000
Net project cost	$1,200,000
Federal share (2/3 of net cost)	$800,000
Local share (1/3 of net cost)	400,000
(Less) Assume local non-cash grants-in-aid	200,000
Cash locality must contribute to project	$200,000

Three-quarters Grant Basis

A project capital grant is based upon three-fourths of the net project cost in a municipality having a population according to the most recent decennial census of:
1. 50,000 or less
2. More than 50,000 but located in an economic development area designated by the Department of Commerce

EXAMPLE OF 3/4 GRANT BASIS

Gross project cost	$2,000,000
(Less) receipts from sale of land	800,000
Net project cost	$1,200,000
Federal share (3/4 of net cost)	$900,000
Local share (1/4 of net cost)	300,000
(Less) assume local non-cash grants-in-aid	200,000
Cash locality must contribute to project	$100,000

Three-quarters Grant on a Limited Cost Basis

A project capital grant may also be based on three-quarters of net project cost (regardless of population size of the municipality) if carried out on a limited cost basis. Item 1 costs are allowable costs payable out of an approved project budget. If the municipality chooses to exclude certain otherwise allowable item 1 costs from the project budget and pay these costs out of its own funds rather than from project funds, the municipality could then undertake the project on a three-quarters grant basis.

Excluded costs must include surveys, planning, administrative, legal, and certain other project expenses in order to qualify on this basis (see 7218.1, chap. 2, sec. 2). It is generally not advantageous for a municipality to use this method except under certain special circumstances.

Supplemental Grants in Model City Areas

In addition to the regular federal grant for urban renewal, a project or projects located in a Model City area approved by HUD may receive a supplemental federal grant or grants up to eighty percent of the local share of the project costs.

EXAMPLE OF SUPPLEMENTAL GRANT

Assume the example of 3/4 grant basis previously shown was located in a Model City area:

Net project cost	$1,200,000
Federal share (3/4 of net cost)	900,000
Local share (1/4 of net cost)	300,000
(Less) supplemental grant (80% of $300,000)	240,000
Revised local share	$ 60,000

RELOCATION AND REHABILITATION PAYMENTS

The sharing of costs outlined above does not include relocation payments to displaced project relocatees or rehabilitation payments to eligible project occupants who rehabilitate their property in accordance with project standards. These payments made by the LPA are reimbursed in full by the Federal Government.

STATE GRANTS

Several states also make grants to the municipalities to defray a portion of the project costs. These state grants are generally applied against the local share, thus further reducing the financial burden of the municipality in its urban renewal project activities.

POOLING CREDITS

The municipality may provide its share of the project cost in cash, or non-cash local grants-in-aid, or both. The excess value of non-cash local grants-in-aid above the municipality's share of the costs for one project may be carried over to another project in the municipality as a pooling credit.

EXAMPLE OF POOLING CREDIT

Assume that a new elementary school constitutes the city's non-cash local grant-in-aid for a project. Fifty percent of the children who attend the school are from the project area.

Cost of school	$1,400,000
Non-cash credit for school	700,000
(Cost of school x percentage of benefit to project)	
Assumed net project cost	$2,400,000
Federal share (3/4 grant basis)	1,800,000
Local share (1/4 grant basis)	600,000
Excess non-cash credit	
($700,000 minus $600,000)	100,000
Eligible credit for pooling to other project	$ 100,000

For limitation of pooling credits between conventional projects and NDP, see 7385.1, chap. 2, sec. 1.

FUNDS FOR SURVEY AND PLANNING

The Federal Government will advance funds to cover necessary expenditures for survey and planning activities in preparation of an urban renewal project. The municipality must use its own funds, however, for a project contemplated to be executed on a three-fourths basis with limited project cost. The total amount of a planning advance must not exceed the expenditures of the LPA which are necessary and in conformance with a HUD approved survey and planning budget in carrying out the activities for which the advance is made (see 7218.1, chap. 1).

Funds will be advanced only pursuant to a contract for planning advance executed by the LPA and the Federal Government after approval of a survey and planning application (see 7206.1, chap. 1, sec. 1). A planning advance must be repaid with interest from any funds, whether federal or local, which become available for undertaking the project, as soon as funds become available to the LPA and before any other expenditures are made. This repayment generally occurs when funds become available for project execution activities.

chapter 4

Planning

RELATIONSHIP BETWEEN COMMUNITY AND PROJECT PLANNING

Urban renewal project planning is, in effect, an extension of community planning in that the plans of an urban renewal area should generally conform to the comprehensive or master plan of the community. On the other hand, as the plans of a project area generally involve more detailed studies and surveys than are required in the preparation of the community's comprehensive plan, the project plans may, to some degree, modify the concepts embodied in the comprehensive plan.

Whereas comprehensive planning tends to be of a more conceptual nature blended with a degree of realism and based upon the community as it exists, project planning develops specific plans and proposals. The comprehensive plan usually shows the general location of proposed public facilities such as schools and playgrounds. The project plans pinpoint the locations of such facilities in the project area. Many of the proposals contained in the comprehensive plan of the community may never be implemented, whereas approval of the urban renewal plans of the project include also approval of the methods and means to implement and finance the project plans and proposals during the project execution stage or in NDP action years.

In many communities urban renewal was the prime motivation toward comprehensive planning due to Workable Program requirements. In many other communities comprehensive planning was a long established and accepted activity of local government, prior to the availability of federal funds for urban renewal.

For years, many communities contracted for the preparation of comprehensive plans by consultants, only to have them gather dust on the proverbial shelf because the community did not employ a planning staff to update or work toward the implementation of the plans. Federal financial assistance in planning and urban renewal was often the needed incentive to get the plans off the shelf. Urban renewal was thus the motivating force or the basic factor in the resurgence of community planning activities throughout the United States.

The nature of urban renewal activities requires a close liaison between the community planners and the LPA director and staff. The project planners may or may not be the community planners, depending on the size and organizational structure of the community and the LPA.

In larger cities, the city planning staff may also do the project planning or the LPA may employ its own staff planners and/or planning consultants. Smaller cities are often unable to employ a resident planning staff and usually utilize only the services of a planning consultant. In the latter case the LPA director often acts as liaison between the city, the planning commission, and the consultant.

The LPA director, in addition to actively participating in or supervising project planning, should have an active interest in community-wide planning. He should maintain a close relationship with the community planners, be fully aware of the various studies under way or contemplated, and be prepared to make recommendations concerning them. On the other hand, the director should keep the planners informed concerning the progress of the projects and potential developments that would have an impact beyond the project boundaries.

In smaller communities the LPA may be the sole repository of all planning reports, studies, and related documents. Whether the city is large or small, the LPA should maintain community planning files. These may include base, plat, and zoning maps; zoning ordinance; subdivision regulations; plans and studies concerning economic base, population, geography, land use, transportation, parks and recreation, community facilities, housing quality, etc.

In a larger city, where these records would be too voluminous to maintain in the LPA offices, only basic reports and studies need be kept there in addition to those specifically applicable to blighted areas of the city. Applicable regional and county planning material should also be kept by the LPA to the extent feasible.

PROJECT PLANNING: CONVENTIONAL PROJECT

7207.1

The survey and planning stage of an urban renewal project requires a great deal of cooperation and coordination between the planners and the LPA director. Generally one of the first steps in project planning is the preparation of the property map. This is usually prepared from ownership data obtained from a title company or the tax maps of the community. Preparations for obtaining this information must be made prior to HUD approval of the Survey and Planning application. Immediately upon approval thereof the necessary contracts should be signed, or other arrangements made to obtain information as quickly as possible.

While this work is proceeding, the structural quality survey should be initiated in order to determine the nature and quality of the buildings and their use and occupancy. If the total project or substantial segments of the project obviously require clearance, then surveys of the occupants of these areas should be made to determine the incomes, family characteristics, and other information necessary to determine their relocation needs. Upon completion of the structural quality surveys, tentative determinations can be made concerning which structures, if any, should remain, and which structures are so dilapidated or deteriorated as to be economically unfeasible to rehabilitate. Tentative determinations should also be made concerning property that should be acquired for planning purposes or because it is a blighting influence, streets and alleys that appear desirable to vacate, or new streets to dedicate, and other similar planning proposals.

Based upon these findings and the project objectives, tentative plans and proposals can be developed for the project area. These would include land use and treatment, relocation, and financing. As these plans and proposals are in the process of formulation, they should be discussed with the LPA director and interested citizens (see chapter 16 for citizens' role in project planning).

As project planning starts, arrangements should be made to obtain a Land Utilization and Marketability Study (LUMS). The basic purpose of the study is "to provide a realistic basis for the formulation of the urban renewal plan" (7214.1, chap. 2). This will provide opportunity for a continuing interplay between the planner and the real estate consultant. Tentative plans and proposals should be discussed with the mayor and governing bodies of the LPA and of the community, if separate entities.

A midplanning conference should then be arranged with the HUD representatives to identify and resolve any significant problems through informal discussions.

As soon as determinations are made concerning property to be acquired, contracts should be entered into for the first acquisition appraisals. As the project plans are being finalized and the controls and restrictions contained in the urban renewal plan completed, authorization to proceed with the reuse appraisals can be granted by the LPA or reuse estimates may be developed by the LPA staff or consultants. Engineering data and cost estimates should be obtained for proposed site improvements including streets, sidewalks, curbs, sewers, water lines, and other facilities to be constructed in the project area.

Upon accumulation of all the necessary data and the compilation thereof, including all costs and local non-cash grants-in-aid, determinations are made concerning the sharing of project costs as part of the financing plan.

Upon completion of the required studies, surveys, urban renewal plan, and other necessary documentation, the required HUD forms are filled out, prepared in the format prescribed by HUD, and inserted in binders as Part I, Loan and Grant Application (see 7207.1, chap. 5, sec. 2 and 3; 7206.1, chap. 2, sec. 1; and appendices 1-4).

In addition to the midplanning conference with HUD staff, further conferences may be necessary before submission of Part I. In residential reuse, project planning conferences should be held as applicable with HUD mortgage insurance specialists, local housing authority, and other low or moderate income specialists. Discussions with project residents, business firms, and knowledgeable developers can also be of some assistance in formulating plans and proposals. When these are completed, the plans and proposals are then submitted to the governing body of the LPA, if a separate entity, and to the governing body of the community for approval following public hearing. Upon approval, the required documentation is then submitted to HUD for approval.

The LPA should retain all survey data, working papers, research, and other material required in project planning, including condition of buildings, basis of determining project eligibility, proposed clearance, and relocation. If any part of the data is compiled by a consultant, the LPA should require that the materials become the property of the LPA at the completion of the contract.

PROJECT PLANNING: NEIGHBORHOOD
DEVELOPMENT PROGRAM

7384.1, chap. 1

The urban renewal planning requirements for a NDP urban renewal area are generally less specific and detailed than for a conventional project. Where appropriate, planning standards and criteria have been substituted for specific and detailed restrictions and maps required in the urban renewal plan for a conventional project. Initial preparation of the physical plan for an urban renewal area included in the NDP is similar in degree of detail to that normally applied to a comprehensive plan of a community. As the program progresses, the level of planning will become more detailed and explicit, but such planning should take place as close to the time of actual execution as possible. The specific plans for the development of the NDP renewal area or portions thereof need not be made part of the urban renewal plan unless state or local law or the unique character of the area requires otherwise.

Except for areas in which only planning activities are programmed for the action year (see 7383.1, chap. 1), an urban renewal plan shall be submitted with the NDP application that proposes the inclusion of a redevelopment area or areas in the program.

Since planning and execution activities will take place concurrently in NDP, it is essential that those responsible for planning work closely with those responsible for redevelopment. In lieu of specific standards and criteria contained in the urban renewal plan for a conventional project, the planning standards and criteria contained in the NDP urban renewal plan will be found in many instances in the community's comprehensive plans or various other development guides such as performance-type zoning ordinances and subdivision regulations.

Prior to submission of the initial NDP application, an NDP Preparatory Conference should be scheduled with the HUD staff to review proposed area boundaries, feasibility of general plan proposals, acceptability of various eligibility findings, and scheduling of planning and execution activities during the first NDP year. Similar conferences should be scheduled prior to submission of subsequent NDP applications.

Where state or local urban renewal enabling legislation does not permit renewal to take place as prescribed in the basic approach to NDP, an alternate approach has been developed (see 7384.1, chap. 1, sec. 1, appendices 1 and 2). Under the alternate apprach the NDP is carried out on the basis of a series of small conventional urban renewal plans, which, over a period of time, implement renewal in the larger urban renewal area covered by a Development Plan. Though the development plan is not an official urban renewal plan, it will serve as a guide in evaluating and relating urban renewal plans for each separate urban renewal area covered by the development plan.

PROJECT PLANNING FILES

Maintain the following files:
1. Eligibility — Keep all surveys and data regarding project and NDP eligibility, including basis of boundary determinations
2. Flooding — If the area is or may be subject to flooding, basis of proposed solutions to problem
3. Water pollution — If proposed renewal in the area will increase pollution load of the sewers, basis of proposed action to treat sewage effectively
4. Minority group considerations — Studies and surveys
5. Low and moderate housing considerations — Studies and surveys
6. Coordination with highway programs — All relevant data concerning county, state, and federal highway plans and proposals affecting the project area
7. Clearance and redevelopment — Studies and basis of proposed redevelopment including LUMS and Economic and Market Analysis Study (EMAS) reports
8. Rehabilitation — Studies, surveys, and data supporting the removal and spot clearance of buildings in a rehabilitation area because:
   a. They are economically unfeasible to rehabilitate;
   b. Their removal eliminates a blighting influence;
   c. Of the necessity to provide land for project improvements or supporting facilities;
   d. Their removal achieves objectives of the urban renewal plan
9. Relocation — Studies and surveys required to obtain necessary data concerning relocatees and their needs and how these needs can be met
10. Historic preservation — (if applicable) — All data relevant to the proposed preservation of historic structures

11. Air rights (if applicable) — All data concerning the proposed disposal of air rights
12. Urban renewal plan — All information and documentation required for the preparation of the urban renewal plan not included in the above categories
13. Urban renewal plan changes — All information and documentation necessary to support the urban renewal plan change
14. Development plan — All information and data necessary if the alternate approach is taken for a NDP
15. Engineering — Studies, surveys, reports, and cost estimates
16. Property acquisition — Appraisals or estimates of property acquisition costs
17. Property disposition — Reuse appraisals or estimates of real property disposition proceeds
18. Fiscal data — Including basis and calculation of costs not included in the above
19. Conference reports — Summaries of all conferences with planners, technicians, and others involved in decision-making concerning project plans and proposals
20. Other related information and data

NOTE:

Upon entering the project execution stage or whenever necessary during the NDP action year, relevant material, such as acquisition or reuse appraisals, may be removed from the project planning files and inserted in the applicable project execution files.

COMMUNITY PLANNING FILES

Maintain the following files to the extent feasible:
1. Comprehensive plan of community, including the following plan elements:
   a. Economic resources
   b. Population
   c. Geography
   d. Design
   e. Land use
   f. Transportation — circulation
   g. Community facilities
2. Zoning ordinance and maps together with all revisions

3. Capital improvements program together with data concerning improvements completed and in process
4. Applicable county and/or regional plans
5. Special planning and zoning studies
6. Community Renewal Program (CRP) plans and documentation
7. GNRP and documentation relating thereto
8. State and federal local planning assistance data
9. City codes and ordinances including building, housing, plumbing, electrical codes, etc.

chapter 5

Local Public Agency Administration

GENERAL MANAGEMENT PRACTICES

The administration of an urban renewal program is a complex undertaking involving many disciplines. The success or failure of any complex undertaking is generally dependent upon the caliber of its management and the management practices of the organization.

Many LPA's with competent staff personnel often fall down in the areas of planning, programming, scheduling, and budgeting. Activities should be scheduled both on a short-term and long-term basis, otherwise the project drags on needlessly. The long duration of many urban renewal projects throughout the country is a stark reminder of the weakness or absence of effective management systems.

MANAGEMENT SYSTEM

A management system is the method by which an organization plans, operates, and controls its activities to meet its goals and objectives. An effective management system depends upon

    a. The expertise of the project's management in planning, scheduling, and budgeting the project activities

    b. The ability of staff personnel to carry out the various project activities or operations in a timely and effective manner

    c. Monitoring project activities and regularly reviewing progress

    d. Timely revision of schedules and budgets when project progress review shows the necessity thereof

One of the earliest, simplest, and most widely used tools for graphic-representation of time schedules and activity progress is the Gantt Chart, developed by Henry L. Gantt, a World War I engineer, to expedite defense shipbuilding. Today it is widely used in many variations for progress planning and controls.

There are three major ingredients in the Gantt Chart: (1) The top row consists of dates and units of time projecting progress. (2) Vertically shown on the left side are units of scheduled results in terms of tangible numbers. (3) Provision for parallel posting of actual achieved results by dates for comparison with the projected progress.

Another, but more complex graphic representation of progress planning is known as a PERT (Program Evaluation and Review Technique) diagram. This method was originally adopted by firms engaged in defense contract work in the early 1960's through Defense Department pressure. This method has gained wide acceptance in manufacturing, construction and other endeavors.

The PERT diagram consists of the interlinking of the various activities by a series of arrows and circles between related or dependent activities, with the probable time periods of each activity shown at the arrow, after the network has been constructed. The arrow represents the activity and the circle is the connecting link between the activities. Activities being carried out simultaneously are indicated by parallel arrows. Sequential activities, or those where starting one depends on the other, are usually indicated by diagonal arrows, or extensions of previous arrow activity. Once the network is completed with time estimates, a determination of the critical path should be made. The critical path is the chain of activities which would require the shortest period to obtain the desired result — in the case of urban renewal, project completion. If any one of the activities along the critical path were delayed, the whole project would be delayed.

Although some attempts have been made to utilize PERT in urban renewal projects, an adaptation of the Gantt Chart has been recommended in this book. See Appendix 8 — Project Progress Schedule No. 1, and Appendix 9 — Project Progress Schedule No. 2.

The reasons for recommending the Schedule shown in Appendices 8 and 9 rather than PERT are as follows:

1. It is simple to prepare, easy to explain to and understand by laymen and project technicians.

2. It is simple to revise if necessary (as shown in Appendix 9), and can be done by the average urban renewal director without the necessity of obtaining professional assistance.

3. It appears to be the more valid approach for most urban renewal projects.

In any event, the installation of an effective management system in an urban renewal program should reap rich rewards to the local community.

PHASING PROJECT ACTIVITIES

Proper phasing of project activities is one of the most important fundamentals of a successful project. The Application for Loan and Grant (Form H-612) requires preparation of a time schedule for starting and completing certain major project activities. This schedule should be realistic and prepared with due deliberation of the nature of the project, the competence and abilities of staff personnel, and prior project experience.

PROJECT PROGRESS REVIEW

7219.1

One of the most widespread and valid criticisms of urban renewal is the long period of time which usually elapses between the start of execution stage activities and project closeout. Constant vigilance of project activities for conformance with established time schedules is a necessary part of a well organized program.

HUD requires periodic reports of the progress of each project. These include Report on Status of Land Acquisition; Disposition and Redevelopment (Form H-6163); Report on Relocation of Families and Individuals (Form HUD-666); Report on Relocation of Business Firms and Non-Profit Organizations (Form HUD-666A); and Physical Progress Report (Form HUD-6000).

The reports are desirable means of recording the status of the various project activities, but they do not provide a yardstick to measure the progress of the activities in relation to the established schedules or goals of the LPA. In fact, the specialists or technicians administering their respective phases of the project are frequently unaware of the existence of these schedules. Many directors regard them as necessary evils required by HUD and promptly ignore them when a project proceeds in the execution stage.

GRAPHIC SCHEDULE

A graphic representation of the time schedules together with a graphic representation of activity progress should be maintained on a monthly or quarterly basis. This provides the LPA with the means to review periodically its own progress, pinpoint any lags or deficiencies in its program, and at the same time, display to the various activity specialists the effect their progress or lack of progress has on other phases of the program (see Appendix 8: Project Progress Schedule No. 1; Appendix 9: Project Progress Schedule No. 2).

QUALIFICATIONS OF THE DIRECTOR

The diverse nature of the urban renewal program requires that a director have unique qualifications. He should possess a good basic education and be a person of good judgment. He should have a general knowledge of real estate, government finance, law, engineering, construction, planning, accounting, public relations, intergovernmental relations, public administration, and urban renewal regulations and procedures. He must have the ability to get along well with people of all economic and social strata.

The renewal director must be a person of superior integrity dedicated to the cause of community and human improvement. He must be able to organize, lead, and generate enthusiasm. He should have foresight, and be able to analyze details quickly without getting bogged down in them. He should possess warmth and understanding, yet be able to maintain a degree of objectivity. He should be able to maintain his "cool" even under the most trying circumstances.

The selection of a competent director is one of the most difficult duties that a LPA governing body or city manager has. Some cities attempt to equate the director on a par with other city department heads, and establish his salary level accordingly. Failure to compensate him adequately could result either in obtaining the services of a second-rate director or in a rapid change of directors who seek greener pastures. Cities that recognize the broad knowledge and special skills required for this important position can usually acquire and keep a competent director by providing an adequate salary, generally above the level paid to other department heads whose scope of services are of a more limited nature.

An able director with a keen eye to potential non-cash credits, timely investments of unutilized project funds, and prudent phasing of project activities that result in a quick return of acquired properties to the tax rolls and reduction of administrative costs can save the city sums far beyond his salary.

THE ROLE OF THE DIRECTOR

In a community with a major urban renewal program, the director primarily functions as an administrator. He would normally have under his supervision activity specialists who direct various segments of a project. They in turn would have subspecialists or line employees under their supervision. The director may also have project coordinators, public relations advisors, and other assistants to help implement and coordinate project activities. The director is the major decision maker, subject to policy determinations of the governing body. He is also the major liaison between the governing body, HUD and other governmental entities, and contractor consultants.

In a smaller program the director is also the major decision maker, liaison officer, and supervisor, but he may also act as the program coordinator, handle public relations and similar activities, and be closer to line activities due to smaller staff or less knowledgeable specialists.

In a community with a small program or a single project, the director, in addition to all other responsibilities, may also handle in its entirety such line functions as acquisition, disposition, or property management, and/or be required to train others in these activities.

ADMINISTRATIVE PRACTICES

7217.1, chap. 1, sec. 4

As soon as possible the LPA shall establish policies and regulations governing administrative practices in conformance with HUD requirements. This would include salary and wage rates for employees, employee fringe benefits, regulations governing travel expenses and reimbursements for the use of privately owned vehicles, and expenses for meetings, publications, and memberships in organizations. Eligibility of costs incurred and conformance with the adopted policies and regulations will be determined pursuant to the periodic audit by HUD of the LPA records.

APPLICATIONS

Petition to the Federal Government for loan and grant assistance is in the form of various applications. Submission of extensive additional documentation is generally required in addition to the particular application form.

URBAN RENEWAL APPLICATIONS INCLUDE:

1.	Survey and Planning	7206.1, chap. 1, sec. 1, 2
2.	Part I: Loan and Grant	7206.1, chap. 2, sec. 1
3.	Part II: Loan and Grant	7206.1, chap. 2, sec. 2
4.	NDP	7382.1, chap. 1
5.	Amendatories (Revision of approved applications)	
	a. Loan and Grant	7206.1, chap. 2, sec. 1
	b. Loan and Grant Financial	7215.1, chap. 1, sec. 2

Although the *Urban Renewal Handbook* appears to require full conformance with the prescribed checklist documentation for an amendatory, actually it is generally necessary to provide revised documentation only for those items affected or revised by the proposed changes. Prior to the preparation of an amendatory application, it is desirable to advise the HUD regional office of such intent and obtain approval thereof before proceeding, and to obtain a determination as to the nature of the documentation necessary to submit. A plan change may not require a full amendatory unless it involves a change in project boundaries, or other major revisions.

The cost of preparing Survey and Planning and NDP applications must be born by the LPA, and are not eligible project costs.

Each application, together with supporting data, should be kept in a separate file folder.

Approval of an application does not incur any financial obligation on the part of either the LPA or the government. The financial obligation is incurred only through the execution of a contract between the parties.

CONTRACTS

A contract is an agreement between two or more parties. All contracts entered into by the LPA should be in writing and duly authorized by resolution or motion in the official minutes of a meeting of the governing body of the LPA. HUD contract guide forms should be utilized to the extent feasible.

A LPA will normally be involved in four types of contracts:

1.	With another government entity, such as a Loan and Grant contract with the United States government.	
2.	Contracts for professional and technical services.	7217.1, chap. 2

3. Site clearance, project improvements,
and similar contracts.   7209.1, chap. 4, sec. 3
4. Contracts for the purchase and
sale of property.   7208.1, chap. 4, sec. 2
                                                7214.1, chap. 4, sec. 3

A running record should be kept of each contract for work or services. This should include the name of the contractor, nature of contract, date executed, contract amount, dates and amounts of payments made, with a running record of balance due. If contract is completed, note accordingly and the date paid in full. If maximum amount is not utilized, note accordingly. If time is an essential part of the contract, such as a contract for appraisal services, specified completion date should also be noted.

Contracts for professional and technical services are generally negotiated. Site clearance, project improvements, and similar contracts are generally awarded on the basis of competitive bidding.

A proposed contract which includes legal services involving litigation shall be submitted to the HUD regional office for concurrence prior to execution. Proposed contracts for site clearance or project improvements would usually be submitted to HUD for approval as part of the bid documents. Prior to the award of the contract, the LPA should receive the approval of the contractor and the contract amount from HUD. Other contracts generally need not be submitted to HUD for approval.

A separate file folder should be maintained for each contract. Contracts should be kept together by subject (i.e., legal, planning, appraisal, etc.). Contracts for the purchase and sale of property should be kept in the appropriate parcel folder.

In addition to file and project numbers, the type of contract, contractor, and subject as shown below should be noted on the tab of the folder:
Legal — Survey & Planning — John Jones
Legal — Execution — John Jones
Legal — Condemnation — William Smith
Legal — Litigation — George Brown
    State Electric Co. vs. City

INSURANCE AND BONDING
7217.1, chap. 4

Close attention should be paid to HUD requirements. If the LPA does not comply with such requirements for insurance and bonding coverages, to the extent of the deficiency of coverage, no uninsured losses, or the expenses in connection therewith, can be included in project costs.

Prior to obtaining HUD required insurance or bonding coverage, the LPA should ascertain whether or not the required coverage is maintained by the city, thus eliminating a duplication of costs. For example, if officials are check signers and countersigners for both the city and LPA, and through their city capacity already have adequate bonding to meet HUD requirements, it would not be necessary to duplicate these coverages.

The LPA should keep an up-to-date record of each policy and bond, showing the carrier, policy number, type of coverage, amount of coverage, amount of premium, effective date, and expiration date.

Certified copies of all policies or bonds charged as a project expense must be submitted to HUD for approval. If satisfactory, the LPA will receive an approval slip which is to be attached to the policy.

For each project a summary of changes in exposures, on a monthly basis, under Owners, Landlords, and Tenants Liability Insurance should be kept by the LPA on HUD Form H-6145. A copy of each completed form is provided the insurance company so that it can make its final adjustment for the premium year. Within 30 days after the expiration of the policy year, the completed form or forms are then sent to the HUD regional office together with the final premium statement of the insurance company. These are then checked and the LPA advised concerning the correctness of the premium.

All LPA policies, bonds, and documentation relating thereto should be kept in the administrative files unless the coverage is already maintained by the city. In that event they may be kept in the files of the public official who normally has custody thereof, with either a certified copy in the LPA files or a memo containing the pertinent information.

Bonds and other evidence of insurance coverage of contractors are normally kept in the contract files together with other contract documentation of the particular contractor.

LABOR STANDARDS:
EQUAL EMPLOYMENT OPPORTUNITY

7217.1, chap. 3;

7203.1

It is the duty of the LPA administrator to assure himself that the federal labor standards provisions are strictly adhered to. These provisions apply to salary and wage rates, fringe benefits, hours of work, kickbacks, classifications of labor, qualifications for employment, overtime, health and safety, equal employment opportunity, and other related matters concerning employment of contractors, subcontractors, and their labor.

These provisions are usually applicable where the contract amount exceeds $2,000. HUD provides the LPA with guide forms for the language to be inserted in the contracts. Following the execution of a loan and grant contract (and subsequent to a determination under state or local law, if applicable), HUD will make a determination of the minimum salaries which may be paid to technical persons employed on the project. These will include planners, architects, engineers, draftsmen, surveyors, etc. This determination, unless later revised, must be made part of each contract involving the employment of such persons.

Prior to advertising for bids on contracts requiring the employment of laborers and mechanics, the LPA should submit to HUD a written request for determination of the prevailing wage rates as determined by the Department of Labor. The request should be made to HUD approximately 45 days prior to the date of advertising and becomes obsolete 120 days after the date of the determination, unless the contract or contracts are awarded within that time. This determination must be made part of each contract. Wage rates and other required information must be posted on the job site. Periodically HUD may submit this information to the LPA without request. If the effective dates have not expired, no further request in wage determination is necessary.

The LPA shall obtain from each contractor and subcontractor one certified copy of each payroll covering the particular job on form HUD-1 and review it to insure compliance with the determined wage rates. Other affirmative actions which the LPA shall take include preconstruction conferences to explain the contract labor standards provisions, random interviews with laborers and mechanics to ascertain whether they are receiving the wages as certified by the contractor, and submission of reports of complaints or non-compliance to HUD.

The executed copy of the contract, together with the determination of prevailing wages, should be kept in the contract files. A copy thereof, together with certified payrolls and information concerning all other affirmative actions taken relative to the particular contract, should be kept in the demolition, site clearance, site improvement, or other applicable file.

It is federal policy to prohibit discrimination in employment because of race, color, religion, sex, or national origin. This policy applies to all LPA contracts or agreements for site clearance, project improvements, rehabilitation work undertaken by the LPA, disposition of project land for private redevelopment or to a public body, construction on project land retained by the LPA, or subcontracts under any of these.

Equal employment requirements are also part of the Federal labor standards.

BUDGETS AND BUDGET CONTROL

7218.1

Close attention to budgetary limitations is a basic ingredient of good administration. Although HUD requires the submission of a semiannual report on budgetary status of projects in execution, together with a balance sheet, it is desirable that a monthly operating summary for each project be prepared and submitted to the urban renewal director for review. This will greatly assist the staff and the director in checking expenditures on a month-to-month basis to insure against budget overruns and/or to determine whether a budget revision is necessary.

Where persons are employed on a project part-time or where the time of various persons is divided between several projects, close attention should be given to the time devoted by such persons to each project to reflect accurately the correct percentage of time. The length and percentage of time that the budget estimates provided for such services should be reviewed regularly to prevent substantial budget overruns.

The project administrator and controller or bookkeeper should work closely together to insure that expenditures are debited against the proper account, i.e., acquisition expenses should not be charged as real estate purchases.

Certain line items of an approved budget may be overobligated to some degree based upon prevailing HUD policy. Other line items may not be overobligated in any amount. Amounts provided for contingencies shall not be used to offset any overrun in an approved activity classification without prior HUD approval. If there is any doubt concerning an actual or potential budget overrun, the applicable provisions of the *Urban Renewal Handbook* should be reviewed. If there is still any doubt, the HUD regional office should be consulted about the desirability of a budget revision. Failure to take timely action could result in an audit finding.

In addition to the project budget, the LPA shall submit for HUD approval an Annual Administrative Staff Expense Budget. Not later than 60 days prior to the beginning of each budget year, the LPA should submit a new Annual Administrative Staff Expense Budget.

An approved NDP Expenditures Budget establishes the total amount of program costs which will be accepted by HUD in computing the federal grants earned during the action year covered by the approved budget. Money for budgeted costs will be derived from cash local grants-in-aid, direct loans from the United States Government and private loans guaranteed by the Federal Government. Obligations or costs incurred for NDP activities during a period not covered by an approved NDP budget will not be eligible for inclusion in NDP costs.

LPAs that conduct only NDP activities are required to submit a modified Annual Administrative Staff Expense Budget. If such a budget was previously approved for a converted project or projects, the budget should be adjusted to coincide with the NDP action year. LPAs that conduct conventional urban renewal projects, low rent public housing, or other activities in addition to NDP activities, need not adjust their budgets to the NDP action year.

The budget files should contain the following, together with related documentation:

1. Each approved project budget and budget revision.
2. Each proposed revision as submitted to HUD.
3. Each NDP budget.
4. Each Annual Administrative Staff Expense Budget.
5. Monthly Operating Summaries.
6. Semiannual reports to HUD.

INVENTORY: DISPOSITION OF PERSONAL PROPERTY

7221.1, chap. 2, sec. 4;

7217.7, chap. 1, sec. 7

Records of all furniture, fixtures, and equipment should be maintained on a continuous basis. This should include identification of article by type; name of manufacturer; serial number, if any; date of purchase; vendor; and cost, together with an assigned inventory number, as shown below, for each project.

#1 — Typewriter — IBM — 1374692 — Ace Office Supply — $432 — 10/24/65

#2 — Desk — National — 246731 — Tops Furniture — $324 — 10/27/65

#3 — Side Chair — National — No Ser. # — Tops Furniture — $87 — 10/27/65

For further identification, the assigned number and project number should be taped on each piece of furniture, fixture, and equipment.

Any article no longer needed by the LPA shall be disposed of in accordance with *Urban Renewal Handbook* requirements. If a particular project is closed out, or the article is no longer needed for use by the project for which it was purchased but can be used for another project of the LPA, the LPA could retain same by transferring it to the account of the assigned project, and depositing to the original project a sum equal to the fair value of the property.

Records should also be kept of equipment warranties, maintenance contracts, and other related material.

AUDITS

7217.1, chap. 1, sec. 1;

7222.1, chap. 1

Approximately every 12 to 18 months, HUD auditors audit the books and records of the LPA at the agency's offices. No prior notice of the auditor's visit is given to the LPA, consequently it is essential that the books and records be kept in good order at all times. During the audit period, which may take several weeks, the auditor may request certain additional information or documentation that may be essential to the audit and not contained in the project records, or he may recommend that certain actions be taken relative to the books and manner of record keeping by the LPA. Various discussions are held between the auditor, LPA director, bookkeeper, and other agency personnel.

The auditors are generally objective, and make every possible effort not to interfere with the normal routine of the LPA. They may make certain recommendations for the elimination of potential audit findings during the course of the audit.

At the completion of the audit, the auditor will submit to the LPA director a written statement of the various findings that he feels have not been fully and completely resolved. The director is then requested to make a written reply or explanation of each finding and/or the action, if any, that will be taken thereon. Several months later copies of the audit report will be received from HUD, together with recommendations concerning the local actions necessary, as a result of the findings of the auditor. It will also contain comments on the replies of the LPA director that were accepted as resolving the applicable finding, and on the replies that were clearly not adequate. Additional information and/or documentation may be requested to resolve the findings.

Files of the LPA should contain a detailed record of all HUD audits, actions taken with regard to each finding, and all related documentation.

Minimizing Audit Findings

Good records and bookkeeping are essential to the proper operation of an urban renewal program, but it takes constant vigilance of expenditures and knowledge of allowable project costs to minimize audit findings. Unauthorized payments or extra costs resulting from errors or omissions are generally not allowable as a project cost, and must be borne by the local community. For example, payment for real estate above the HUD concurred acquisition price is generally not allowable, nor are expenditures to clear title to property acquired, without first determining that the seller is able to give good title free and clear of liens and encumbrances.

Before the payment of any bills, a check should be made to insure that the goods have been delivered as ordered or the services performed as contracted. Services contracted for on an hourly basis, such as certain legal work, should be paid only after first ascertaining that there is an unpaid balance remaining in the contract, and upon receipt of a detailed breakdown on a day-to-day basis of the nature of the work performed, and the number of hours or portions of hours devoted thereto.

ADMINISTRATIVE FILES

The following files should be maintained depending on the nature of the LPA (i.e., authority, commission, or city) and the scope of its activities:

1. Organization and procedures (if the governing body of the community is *not* the governing body of the LPA):
   a. Resolution or ordinance of the governing body of the community establishing the agency
   b. Information regarding appointment of members of governing body of agency (commissioners), terms of office, expiration dates of terms, etc.
   c. Rules or procedures and/or by-laws
   d. Minutes of meetings, copies of resolutions, etc.

2. Policies and regulations governing administrative practices
3. Project applications and supporting documentation
4. Contracts, resolution authorizing contracts, and related information and documentation
5. Insurance policies and bonds of LPA, claim records, etc.
6. Prevailing wage rate determinations and records of violations by contractors of such wage rates or equal employment provisions of contracts
7. Budget information and reports
8. LPA progress reports including copies of reports to HUD
9. Inventory records
10. Audit reports and related documentation
11. Personnel records
12. Miscellaneous administrative records

chapter 6

Real Estate Acquisition

7208.1; 7384.1, chap. 2

Early determination of property acquisition and related procedures will greatly accelerate project activities. Under certain circumstances, subject to HUD approval, early acquisition can take place prior to the signing of a loan and grant contract for a conventional project. Some acquisition of real estate should normally take place during the NDP action year.

As soon as possible interviews should be held with appraisers, and their qualifications determined and evaluated. Interviews should also be held with representatives of abstract and title companies about obtaining title information necessary for preliminary planning or for a NDP application, and at the same time determine title insurance costs and the cost of related activities that the company can perform during the execution period or the NDP action year. This information, if correlated at an early stage, could reduce the total project costs of such services.

APPRAISALS—ESTABLISHING FAIR VALUE

When the preliminary planning has proceeded to a point that a tentative determination can be made with regard to properties to be acquired, or upon approval of an NDP application, contracts for acquisition appraisals can be entered into.

When Part I of the Loan and Grant application is completed for a conventional project, the LPA should be prepared to enter into the contract for the second acquisition appraisals. These should normally be completed before federal approval of Part II of the Loan and Grant application.

The appraisals should be reviewed to insure that they are properly documented in accordance with good appraisal practices, and that the valuations of both appraisers are generally compatible with each other (usually not exceeding a 15 percent variation). Substantial valuation differences should be resolved by consultation with both appraisers. Under the proclaimer procedure, if the fair value of the propetry under a single ownership does not exceed $100,000, the LPA establishes the value and the appraisals should not be sent to HUD. If the value exceeds $100,000, they should be sent to HUD with Form H-6144 (Request for Concurrence in Acquisition Price).

Upon establishment of fair value or receipt of concurrence from HUD and approval by the LPA governing body (if required by state or local law) offers can be made to property owners. If the Loan and Grant contract has not yet been executed (or if early acquisition has not been granted), the concurrence received, or value established, would be conditional. In that event, only an option may be obtained. Otherwise a firm purchase agreement may be entered into. It is desirable that adequate time be provided for the LPA to exercise the option in order to provide for unforeseen delays.

ACQUISITION PROCEDURES

Acquisition procedures will vary from one LPA to another, depending upon the experience of available personnel. In some cases the LPA staff will perform all of the acquisition functions; in some cases the LPA staff will handle some of the acquisition functions and the project attorney and/or a local realtor who might serve under contract as a negotiator will handle other functions. In other cases the project attorney may handle most of the acquisition functions.

Owners should generally be offered the fair value of the property as established by the LPA under the proclaimer procedures. If the price exceeds $100,000 or the same owner owns several parcels of property in a project of which the total price exceeds $100,000, the LPA may negotiate with the owner by initially offering less than the concurred price.

The single offer policy, if clearly explained to the owner, tends to eliminate long negotiations and differentials of prices offered to several owners of substantially the same type of properties. In no event should a price be offered which exceeds the HUD concurred price or the established fair value.

Prior to actual purchase, a title commitment or other means of assuring a free and clear title should be obtained from a title or abstract company. The owner is required to correct any defects which might appear, as such costs are not allowable project expenses. Care should also be taken to prorate taxes and figure accurately other debits and credits on the closing statement.

Even if the closing statement is prepared by an attorney, the accuracy of the arithmetic should be checked prior to requisitioning or drawing the necessary checks. Costs usually charged against the seller in an ordinary real estate transfer, such as documentary stamps, state or local transfer taxes, preparing releases of mortgages and other encumbrances, and certain other costs, are payable by the LPA in an urban renewal transfer as Settlement Costs, and thus should not be debited against the seller (see 7212.1, chap. 3, sec. 1, appendix 5). These costs are 100 percent reimbursable to the LPA as a project relocation cost.

In the case of rental property, the rent paid to the prior owner should be determined in order to establish the tenant's rent payable to the LPA after acquisition, and to provide a debit on the closing statement against the seller for any portion of the prepaid rent based upon the prior rental agreement. If the owner paid utility costs, meter readings should be made as near as possible to the closing date. Upon closing, relocation and property management personnel should immediately be notified in writing of the completion of the transaction.

Prior to the closing, the person or persons in possession of the property should be interviewed in order to confirm the statement of the owner concerning rent payments (or delinquency) and the actual status of the person in possession. Although the seller may be the record title-holder, the person in possession may be a contract purchaser who failed to record the contract, or a tenant of such contract purchaser. Ownership of major applicances, such as stove, refrigerator, or air conditioner and whether such equipment was included in the appraiser's valuation should be established before purchase.

If the tenant is in possession under a lease which terminates beyond the period necessary for the LPA possession of the property, then a release should be obtained prior to or at the time of closing. Otherwise the LPA would normally get title subject to the lease and might have difficulty in displacing the tenant.

Just prior to closing, the condition of the property should be checked to insure that no major change in the condition of the premises has taken place since the appraisals. If there has been any substantial change such as fire damage or the removal of basic equipment, then the closing should be stopped and the property revalued, based upon the changed condition.

In the case of commercial or industrial property, those fixtures and equipment that were considered as irremovables and the cost thereof included in the property appraisal should be clearly explained to the seller and/or the person in possession. In certain cases where such irremovables are specialized in nature and beyond the ability of the average real estate appraiser to evaluate, it may be necessary to employ the services of a special appraiser of irremovables. HUD approval should first be obtained and the appraisal should generally be made concurrent with the real estate appraisal or shortly thereafter. In establishing fair value or requesting concurrence of HUD in the acquisition price, the real estate valuation plus the irremovable valuation should be taken into consideration.

CHRONOLOGY OF REAL ESTATE ACQUISITION ACTIVITES

1. Interview representatives of title or abstract companies. Obtain information concerning scope of services they can perform, plus the costs thereof.
2. Contract for ownership data and related title services.
3. Interview appraisers and determine their respective qualifications.
4. Contract for acquisition appraisals.
   a. If NDP, both appraisals are made at the same time.
   b. If conventional project, first appraisal is made early in planning period; second appraisal made upon HUD approval of Part I.
5. Compile list of properties to be acquired recording parcel number and address of property; owner of record; contract purchaser, if any; legal description; price established as fair value or price submitted to HUD for concurrence; price concurred in by HUD and tentative priority of acquisition, if any; provide columns for each appraiser's valuation (see Appendix 2).

NOTE:

In compiling the list make certain that all abutting properties owned by the same person or persons are considered as one parcel for the purpose of making an offer to the owner, even if titles to the various properties were acquired at different times. If the original acquisition list listed such parcels separately and/or if the appraisals to such parcels were made separately, they may be combined. For example: if parcels 2-1, 2-2, 2-3 were originally listed separately and/or appraised separately, they should be bracketed together on the list and the fair value established or the request for concurrence submitted for parcels *2-1 to 2-3 inclusive*, on a single line. Tentative priorities should be established, based upon the urgency of areas to be redeveloped and/or the expressed desires of property owners, if they do not conflict with the timing of acquisition activities.

6.   Prepare option form or form of purchase agreement.
7.   Analyze and reconcile appraisals.
8.   Establish fair market value if HUD concurrence not required.
9.   Obtain approval by governing body of proposed offering prices together with authorization to acquire property, if required by state or local law.
10. Submit appraisals to HUD together with Form H-6144, Request for Concurrence in Acquisition Prices, if property value exceeds $100,000.
11. Upon receipt of concurrence by HUD or establishment of fair value by LPA:
     a.   Contact property owner in accordance with established priorities.
     b.   Explain basis of establishment of single offer method (if utilized) and make offer. Explain option or purchase agreement and request signing thereof. Answer all reasonable questions. Be courteous at all times. If after further negotiation an agreement cannot be reached with owner, obtain authorization from governing body to institute condemnation proceedings either singly or on a consolidated basis in accordance with general practice in the area.
12. Closing procedures (see below).
13. After closing, give written notice of change of ownership to assessor, city treasurer, and/or any other official keeper of city tax records, and, if applicable, to utility companies. (If utility is city owned, such as water, and unpaid bill would constitute a lien upon the property, the meter should be read and bill paid prior to closing or a sufficient sum held in escrow to pay same.)

Typical Acquisition Closing:
City of Lincoln Park, Michigan

A.   The Urban Renewal Department will send a cover letter enclosing and notifying the attorney of the following:

1. A copy of the signed Option to Purchase.
2. Address, phone number, and whether tenant or owner occupied or both. (If tenant, submit rent information.)
3. A form signed by owner requesting the mortgage balance owing, if any, to the date of closing. (Date to be filled in by attorney.)
4. Whether or not a water meter reading to date of closing will be necessary.
5. Abstract or title company contract number for project plus commitment number for parcel.

B. Upon receipt of the above forms and information, the attorney will:
   1. Obtain tax information (current and delinquent) from the Wayne County treasurer's office and the treasurer's office of the City of Lincoln Park.
   2. Call or write the seller to set up a closing date in his office. (If tenant is in possession, get rent confirmation.)
   3. Order updated title commitment from the title company as close to date of closing as possible.
   4. Send out request for mortgage balance owed to mortgage holder, requesting pay-off figure to date of closing.
   5. After receiving updated title commitment, call seller and notify him as to what documents he is to bring to the office at time of closing (i.e., paid tax receipts, paid water bills, satisfaction of liens, etc.). If up-dated title commitment indicates any change in ownership, title defects, etc., the department should immediately be advised.
   6. Send the Urban Renewal Department three completed copies of the closing statement showing the proration of taxes, proration of rent, if any, and the checks to be drawn for closing. This should be received by the department at least two days before closing date. The following settlement costs should be shown on the closing statement as chargeable to the city because these are authorized reimbursable expenses under Urban Renewal regulations. The city is then fully reimbursed for these costs by the Federal Government.
      a. Documentary stamps or transfer tax
      b. Preparing and recording releases of mortgages and other encumbrances
      c. Penalty paid by the seller for the prepayment of a mortgage encumbering the property (if any)
      d. Certain other costs incident to transfer of title
   7. Prepare statutory form of warranty deed conveying property to the City of Lincoln Park.

C. When the department receives the completed copies of the closing statement, the department will:
1. Make a final inspection of the property in accordance with HUD regulations. If the property is not appreciably the same as appraised, the department will notify the attorney to stop closing proceedings.
2. Have checks drawn and forwarded to the attorney, together with copies of the closing statement signed by the Urban Renewal director.
3. In the event a water reading is necessary, the Urban Renewal Department will advise the water department to make a meter reading and submit a bill to it. The department will then contact the seller and advise him to come to its office for the purpose of payment of said bill prior to closing.
D. After closing in the attorney's office, the attorney will:
1. Send the department a copy of the signed closing statement and a copy of the Notice to Tenant, if any. The attorney will mail a copy of Notice to Tenant to the tenant, or tenants, occupying the property.
2. Send check to mortgage holder, if any, and request that a discharge of mortgage be mailed to his office.
3. Send the warranty deed and discharge of mortgage to the Register of Deeds office to be recorded along with check for recording fees and revenue stamps.
4. Order a Title Policy to insure the City of Lincoln Park after recorded warranty deed is returned to his office.
5. Forward all the above documents to the Urban Renewal Department along with any paid tax receipts and other documentation related to the transaction.

NOTE:

If contract purchaser is involved in the transaction, all necessary releases, assignments, and/or deed must be obtained in addition to the above documentation.

PROPERTY ACQUISITION FILES

Maintain the following files:
1. Acquisition appraisals (including appraisals of irremovables, if applicable)
2. Requests to HUD for Concurrence in Acquisition Prices (Forms 6144 or 6144A) and data relative to establishment of fair value

3. List of all properties to be acquired (see Appendix 2, Acquisition Parcel Data Form)
4. Maintain a separate file folder for each acquisition parcel. Include in file:
   a. List of all contacts with owners, showing dates and brief summary of discussions
   b. Title commitment
   c. Option (or purchase agreement)
   d. Deed (copy, then recorded deed)
   e. Closing statement
   f. Tax information
   g. Other related information and documentation
5. Information concerning condemnation (include applicable information in each parcel folder)
6. Maintain complete chronology of all acquisition procedures, including dates thereof for each parcel of property (see Appendix 3 — Checklist of Acquisition Procedures)

chapter 7

Property Management

7211.1

Property management is closely related to the relocation and real estate functions of the LPA. It may be carried out as a staff activity, or certain responsibilities may be assigned to another agency or firm by contract. If the work related thereto is assigned by contract, a local housing authority or a real estate firm with such experience is the most logical selection.

Most agencies prefer to handle these activities with their own staffs. There are distinct advantages in retaining property management as a staff activity. These include the establishment and maintenance of a personal relationship between the site occupant and LPA staff, a more sympathetic attitude toward the tenant's problems, and a closer liaison with other staff specialists.

The *Urban Renewal Handbook* generally prescribes the basic principles concerning the administration of the property management program, together with information concerning tenant and related accounting.

The property management function commences upon the acquisition of each parcel of property and to some degree continues until the property is disposed of.

Upon acquisition of the property, the acquisition officer should immediately notify the person responsible for the property management activities and provide applicable information relating thereto. This will generally include the following:

1. Identification of parcel (address and parcel number)

2. Nature of improvements thereon (if any)
3. List of tenants (if tenant occupied)
4. Identification of tenant facilities (apartment number, size, etc.)
5. Previous rental paid including status of leasehold (lease terms or month-to-month), due date of rent payment, credit, if any, for prepaid rent, etc.
6. Nature of facilities, if any, previously supplied (water, gas, electricity)
7. If owner occupied, purchase price thereof (this may be a determining factor in establishing rent to be charged to the previous owner for continued occupancy)

Some of the above information may be contained in the closing statement, a copy of which may also be provided to the property management section.

LEASES OR INFORMATIONAL STATEMENTS

7211.1, chap. 3

As soon as feasible after the property is acquired, the occupants thereof should be offered a lease or handed an informational statement, depending upon local decision. The basic information which must be included therein is contained in 7211.1, chap. 3.

The informational statement (see Appendix 4) is generally preferred because it is a less formal instrument and the site occupant will more readily sign or acknowledge it. Many low income people are suspicious of legal documents; their refusal to sign a lease may create an initial sense of hostility which may be difficult to overcome later.

The informational statement should also contain the basic information and facts concerning relocation assistance that will be available to the site occupant, or an acknowledgement of receipt of a booklet containing facts on relocation. The occupant should retain a copy and sign a copy for the LPA files. Information contained therein should also be explained to the site occupant by the relocation specialist. Should the occupant refuse to sign the copy, no issue over such failure should be made, but the relocation specialist should note thereon the name of the person or persons to whom he gave the information; the facts concerning the refusal to sign, and the date.

The data contained in the informational statement should generally include and/or comply with the tenant policy as adopted by the governing body of the LPA.

PROPERTY MAINTENANCE

7211.1, chap. 1

Until the property is vacated, facilities contained therein should be kept in safe, operating condition. Expenditures for repairs should be kept to the minimum needed to maintain the premises as habitable. If a major expenditure is required due to such factors as irreparable failure of major structural items, e.g., a furnace or heavy damage due to wind or fire, it may be more prudent to move the tenant to another previously vacated property on-site, comparable or better than the prior condition of the one occupied, than to assume the high repair costs.

Vacated property should be protected from vandalism, fire, and unauthorized occupancy. Grass should be mowed, and any maintenance work done whenever necessary to prevent the property from becoming an eyesore to the neighborhood, thus putting the entire program in a negative light. Cleared land should also be maintained. Proper maintenance makes the property more attractive to potential redevelopers and gives a more favorable impression of the area.

It is generally desirable to order the demolition of structures as soon as possible after the property is vacated. However, in a period when displacement activities are very active, it might be prudent to retain several of the better acquired buildings should certain temporary on-site moves become necessary due either to an occupied structure becoming uninhabitable or difficulty in relocating certain site occupants whose retention in existing facilities would adversely affect the redevelopment of a segment of the project.

RENT COLLECTION

7211.1, chap. 3

The LPA should make a diligent effort to collect rent as it becomes due. Failure to take such action will result in a proportionately high ratio of rent delinquencies. A constant check should be made of the rent roll and the tenant's ledger. It is generally desirable to compile form letters to remind the tenant of past-due rent.

The first letter may be in the form of a reminder and should be sent after one week's delinquency. In the event the rent is not paid after approximately two weeks, a second form letter should be mailed to the tenant advising that in the event the rent is not paid within a stipulated period (say 5 days), the matter will be turned over to the project attorney for further action. A personal visit by the relocation specialist or other staff member may be in order at this stage to determine whether illness, unemployment, or other factor was the cause of such nonpayment and would justify deferment of further action.

In the event that at this stage the occupant appears financially capable to meet his rent obligation but apparently refuses to do so, the matter should be referred to the attorney and/or the governing body, together with the applicable information and a recommendation concerning possible eviction action. Firmness at an early stage of the delinquency can eliminate many problems later.

If the tenant were permitted to have his rent fall in arrears for several months, it would often be a great hardship for him to pay it in a lump sum. Knowledge of such permitted delinquency will encourage other tenants to fall behind in their rent payments. Knowledge of firm action, on the other hand, encourages other tenants to pay promptly, which in turn helps in the maintenance of good personal relationships with site occupants.

If the tenant is truly unable to meet his rent obligations, either wholly or partially, then no further action should be taken for the collection thereof, unless his financial status improves prior to relocation. If no such improvement occurs, then such rents should be written off periodically by resolution of the governing body of the LPA.

In order to maintain a close check on rent delinquencies, the LPA director should receive a report regularly (every 2 to 4 weeks) informing him of the status of rents more than two weeks in arrears. Failure to take diligent action in the collection of rents due could result in an audit exception at a later date.

TEMPORARY LEASING TO OFF-SITE TENANTS

7211.1, chap. 2

Under certain circumstances it may be desirable to lease temporarily vacant structures or cleared land to off-site tenants, provided such a lease will either further the objectives of the project, benefit project residents, or minimize hardships, and will not delay or adversely affect project completion. Land or structures may also be leased or used temporarily for social or recreational purposes.

Temporary leases should generally be on a month-to-month basis, with a thirty-day cancellation clause. Any proposed lease that does not contain a thirty-day cancellation clause must receive prior HUD concurrence. Discretion must be used in temporary leasing to off-site tenants, in order to be sure that the proposed use will conform to existing zoning to the extent practicable to the uses permitted by the urban renewal plan, and that it will not be necessary to resort to eviction proceedings in order to remove the tenant.

REAL ESTATE TAX PAYMENTS AND CREDITS

7211.1, chap. 4

Gross project cost, subject to certain limitations and exclusions may include:

(1) Taxes or payment in lieu of taxes on real property owned by the LPA, when required or permitted by state or local law;

(2) Tax credits on real property owned by the LPA, when state or local law does not require or permit tax payments.

Since tax credits are considered to be cash local grants-in-aid, it is important that an accurate record be kept of such credits in conformance with HUD requirements. These credits can often result in a substantial saving of the cash requirements of the community in meeting its share of the project cost (see Appendix 5 for form for tabulating real estate tax payments and credits).

PROPERTY MANAGEMENT FILES

The following files should be maintained:

1. Tenant file: A file folder should be maintained for each tenant. If relocation and property management functions are carried out by the same staff personnel, or if they are closely situated to each other, the relocation and property management sections may utilize the same file folder. The following should be inserted in the file folder:

   a. Notice of occupancy (containing applicable information concerning tenancy; copy to bookkeeper)

   b. Lease or informational statement

   c. Correspondence concerning tenancy

   d. Notice of change in rent (if applicable); copy to bookkeeper

   e. Vacate notice: send to utility companies and others as applicable; copy to bookkeeper (contains information concerning date premises vacated, location of keys thereto necessary for removal of water or gas meters, etc.)

   Depending on the nature of the property in general, copies of rent receipts, utility bills, and repair bills may be kept in the tenant's file folder, or in separate folders kept either by the property management personnel, the bookkeeper, or both. For example, if most of the property acquired is single family residential, the foregoing may be kept in the tenant folder. If most of the property acquired is multi-family residential where repair or utility bills may cover buildings involving several tenants, it would not be feasible or applicable to include this material in the tenant's folder.

2. Tenant ledger
3. Rent roll: Record of total rent chargeable for month and adjusted during the month to reflect changes, moves, etc.; used to make appropriate entries in tenant and project ledgers
4. Key file or key board
5. General correspondence concerning property management
6. Contractor's list (plumbers, electricians, etc., available for property repairs or maintenance)
7. Other files as necessary

chapter 8

Relocation

7212.1

The relocation function is probably the most sensitive aspect of urban renewal. The size of the relocation staff depends upon the size and nature of the program. In larger communities there may be several specialists on the staff who handle certain matters exclusively. These specialists may include trained social caseworkers, persons who concentrate their efforts in obtaining listings of potential relocation resources, business and/or industrial specialists, persons who process moving claims, inspectors of potential housing resources, etc.

In a small or medium sized community, all of these activities may be performed by one or several persons. This person or persons must have a broad knowledge of all aspects of relocation, and at the same time a deep concern for the welfare of people.

The dilemma of the smaller community is that the approved salary schedule generally precludes attracting an experienced person from another community. On the other hand, there are usually few local persons with the combined training and attitude to qualify them for this difficult position.

QUALIFICATIONS OF RELOCATION SPECIALIST

Relocation activity is essentially a real estate function. It requires a knowledge of all aspects of real estate, including sales and rental of residential and business property, property management, and potential relocation resources, including multi-family property owners, realtors, and financial institutions. A good relocation specialist should understand real estate financing in order properly to advise and assist the relocatee. He should also have a knowledge of HUD mortgage insurance programs, Small Business Administration (SBA), Veterans Administration (VA), local welfare, and other governmental agency requirements and procedures.

Due to the sensitive nature of the relocation function, the general tendency of an agency is to seek the services of a trained social worker. Although some social workers have developed into excellent relocation specialists over a period of time, a person with the proper dedication and desire to serve his fellow man and with a knowledge of real estate, could make a substantial contribution to a new or smaller agency from the day that he starts working for the LPA.

RELOCATION SURVEYS

The relation between the relocation specialist and relocatee is personal and intimate; therefore, the services of the specialist should be employed on a project as soon as possible. Generally in the early stages of project planning, surveys are conducted of all site occupants to be relocated to determine income, family size, whether owners or tenants, relocation preferences, and other pertinent information. Surveys are also made to determine the potential availability of future relocation resources. For a community with an existing program, this work should generally be performed by a staff specialist. If the community is entering into its first project activities, the surveys are generally performed on a contract basis by consultants or by the community planners.

In any event, these initial surveys should be updated just prior to entering the project execution stage. The updating of the information gives a current picture of the potential problem cases, reflects changes in the economic conditions, and/or the ownership and tenancies of the site occupants. Equally important, it affords the opportunity to establish a dialogue with these persons. Through the relocation specialist, the relationship with the site occupants becomes more personal.

RELATIONS WITH RELOCATEES AND LISTING SOURCES

Hostility and suspicions of the site occupants can be substantially reduced if the relocation specialist has the proper attitude. He can become an effective liaison between the site occupant and other staff personnel. Very often the confidence he instills in the owner-occupant can establish a less hostile and more positive attitude in negotiations for property acquisition. Advising an eligible owner-occupant of relocation benefits, such as small business displacement payment and relocation assistance payment, may tip the scales in favor of his signing an option even though he may not be satisfied with the price offered for his property.

It is essential that the sources of potential relocation facilities be cultivated. Generally their desires should be respected if they in no way compromise the program or the relocatee. Relations with realtors, landlords, and other listing sources should always be candid and honest. A problem case should not be praised as one of high character and financial responsibility if, in fact, the contrary is known. The time and efforts of a property owner or realtor should not be abused by recommending that the relocatee look at a certain property listed for purchase when obviously the relocatee does not have the financial means to purchase the property. Loss of confidence in the relocation specialist by the realtors or other sources of listings could adversely affect the entire relocation phase of the program and, in fact, the program itself.

On the other hand, referrals from the relocation office could be an excellent source of business for the realtors, but they should generally be treated with impartiality and without favoritism. Good relations with them could be beneficial to all parties concerned.

FUNCTION OF RELOCATION STAFF

The function of the relocation staff should be to *assist* the displaced site occupant in obtaining decent facilities at a price he can afford. He should be encouraged to seek such facilities on his own, but he should also be encouraged to obtain the help of the relocation staff for a physical and financial evaluation of the potential resource before making a firm commitment.

The relocation staff should render such assistance as may be necessary in expediting the actual move. This may vary in each individual case, from making arrangements for the payment of moving expenses to arranging and helping to the smallest detail an elderly widow or a disabled person. The cooperation of the moving firms should be solicited without favoritism.

Although all dwelling facilities should be inspected prior to recommending them or prior to the move, it is usually desirable to visit the dwelling subsequent to the move, both to encourage good public relations and to insure that all basic amenities have been maintained and that the facilities remain in good condition. A record of these inspections should be kept in the appropriate files.

Throughout the entire relationship, the relocatee should be fully apprised of his rights and obligations. It is not sufficient to hand him an informational statement only (see Appendix 4), but the statement and related data should be explained and, if necessary, reexplained to whatever degree is necessary for the particular individual or family to understand.

The degree of assistance necessary for business firms also varies considerably. Large and/or successful business firms may not require or desire any assistance except compensation for moving costs, whereas small or marginal firms may require a great deal of help. This may include finding an adequate and satisfactory place to relocate, assisting in the financing of improvements to the relocation facilities, or any similar financing necessary through the SBA or other sources, and helping in the actual move. If the business firm should decide to terminate operations, assistance should be offered in making arrangements for the liquidation of the business to insure that the individual or firm obtains the maximum funds possible from such liquidation, including the small business displacement payment and payment for direct loss of property, in lieu of moving expenses.

PROPERTY LISTINGS

Property listings are the nucleus of a successful relocation program. Although regular solicitation of local realtors is usually the best source of property listings, the LPA should also subscribe to a central listing agency if maintained by the local real estate board, regularly review real estate advertisements in the local newspapers, and arrange to be placed on the Veterans' Administration (VA) and HUD mailing lists of repossessed properties. The relocation specialist should become acquainted with officials of local banks and other lending institutions, and also with large property owners and landlords.

Even with all these contacts, at times it may be difficult to locate appropriate facilities for a particular family, individual, or business firm at a given time. In that event, the LPA should not hesitate to insert advertisements in the local newspapers for a given type or size of house, apartment, or business property.

RELOCATION FILES

Maintain the following files and records:

1. Relocation surveys
2. Case file: A separate file folder should be maintained for each
   case on the relocation work-load. The various cases having the
   same or similar status should be grouped together and separated
   from cases in a different status. The various groups should be
   divided and identified either by file dividers or by removable
   color tabs. The various classifications should include the following:
   a. Occupants of property at time of signing of Loan and Grant
      Contract or letter from HUD to proceed with project execu-
      tion activities.
   b. Occupants who moved prior to LPA acquiring property
      which they occupied.
   c. Occupants of acquired property still on site.
   d. Occupants satisfactorily relocated, and removed from work-
      load.
   e. Temporary on-site moves.
   f. Temporary off-site moves.
   g. Occupants relocated in substandard facilities — still on work-
      load.
   h. Occupants relocated in substandard facilities — removed
      from work-load.
   i. Occupants who moved too far away to inspect facilities.
   j. Occupants moved; address unknown; still tracing.
   k. Occupants moved; address unknown; tracing efforts futile.
   l. Occupants satisfactorily relocated but still receiving reloca-
      tion assistance or similar payments.

   Each folder in each group should be arranged in alphabetical
   order. When the status of the relocatee changes, the file folder
   should be removed from the prior grouping and placed in the new
   grouping. File folders should not be taken out of the project offices.
3. Card file for relocation specialist's field use should contain brief
   summary of applicable data with space for field notes concerning interviews with relocatee, property referrals, etc.
4. Listing files: Divide by types of facilities (i.e., 1, 2, 3, or 4 bed-
   room rental units or sale housing; commercial; industrial; etc.).

Show location, price or rent, listing realtor or owner. Include inspection records for each listing. When displacee relocates in one of listed properties, insert inspection record and other listing data in relocatee's folder.

5. Record of relocation payment claims and related data.
6. Determination of average annual gross rentals and sales price data for replacement housing payments.
7. Relocation adjustment payment and assistance records.
8. Small business displacement payment records.
9. Relocation reports to regional office of HUD.
10. Forms, informational statements, business and commercial relocation guides, etc.
11. Miscellaneous.

In addition to the above, a control chart (see Appendix 6) should be maintained for instant reference, giving the name, address, status, and other pertinent data of each case.

chapter 9

Demolition and Site Clearance

7209.1, chaps. 2 and 4

The start of the demolition phase of a project is an important and dramatic part of the activities and offers a great opportunity to publicize the objectives and progress of the project. This is especially true in a community involved in its first project.

NATURE OF DEMOLITION AND SITE CLEARANCE ACTIVITY

Demolition and site clearance may be carried out as either an Item I (project expense) or Item II (non-cash, local grant-in-aid) activity. The work may be performed by private contractor or contractors generally on the basis of a competitive bid award or through the utilization of city personnel and equipment (force account). If the latter is the case, detailed records must be maintained of the services performed by each person, equipment charges and the basis thereof, equipment rental, the cost of supplies, such as fill dirt, all moneys received from the sale of salvable items, etc.

PREPARATION OF BID DOCUMENTS

7209.1, chap. 4, sec. 2

Bid documents and related material should be prepared shortly after the project enters the execution stage or as part of a NDP action year activity. Since much of the required documentation is the same or similar to that required for project improvements, it is generally desirable that the same engineer be contracted for the preparation of both at the same time. HUD will provide guide forms for the preparation of the necessary bid documents.

Before preparing the demolition and site clearance specifications, certain local determinations should be made, e.g., if burning should be permitted and if so under what conditions and restrictions, or if certain building removal to another site should be permitted. If it is decided that certain buildings should be removed off-site, prior HUD approval is necessary. To obtain HUD approval a full description of the circumstances under which the buildings are to be moved should be submitted. A determination should also be made whether the removal of same are to be permitted under the demolition contract or whether the buildings are to be offered for sale separately, without any connection with the demolition offering.

After the basic demolition and site clearance documents and specifications are completed, they can be used for later biddings with minor changes, such as inserting the list of additional buildings to be demolished and descriptions thereof, and the latest determination of prevailing wage rates.

One phase of site clearance is closely related to project improvements and, in fact, is generally contracted for with project improvement work. In the reconstruction of such public facilities as streets, sidewalks, and curbs, it is often necessary to remove all or part of the old ones. After streets and alleys are vacated it is necessary to remove the pavements and other improvements.

Bid documents should clearly require unit bids to detail the cost of the various operations. This will also simplify the project bookkeeping because the clearance portion of the work is budgeted as demolition and site clearance expense, and payments therefore should be charged against the applicable account.

COMPLIANCE WITH CONTRACT DOCUMENTS

If the work is performed under contract, care should be taken that the contractor fully complies with the specifications, wage rate provisions, and other applicable provisions of his contract. Provision should be made for almost constant inspection of demolition and site clearance activities, including dumping if done within the community or on community controlled dumps. If burning is permitted, the LPA should be sure there is compliance with the terms of the specifications. If burning is not permitted, the specifications should state so clearly.

Improperly performed demolition and site clearance work could lead to great difficulty and possible lawsuits by developers who may be faced with increased construction costs due to the necessity to remove and replace improper basement fill. Early and excessive settling of buildings may also take place due to such improper basement fill.

MAINTAINENCE OF PROPERTY PRIOR TO DEMOLITION

Vandalism of property slated for demolition is one of the major problems of the LPA. As soon as a building is vacated, it becomes fair game for vandals and petty crooks. Salvable equipment such as sinks, hot water heaters, cabinets, and furnaces are often stolen. Windows are often broken and doors removed. If the building is not removed shortly after being vacated, or if adequate security measures are not taken to prevent this vandalism, the program may be subject to adverse publicity and the further deterioration of the building will quickly accelerate blight conditions in the neighborhood. This could adversely affect the neighborhood rehabilitation efforts, and create a negative image of the area in the minds of potential developers.

In order to arrest the vandalism the police should be alerted to provide the neighborhood with additional surveillance. In some cases it may be necessary for the LPA to employ special security police. It may also be desirable to board up the windows and inspect the premises regularly to be certain doors are locked to prevent unlawful entry.

Unless adequate measures are taken to secure the buildings, they become attractive nuisances to children, winos, and shady characters. The city could become party to a legal action resulting from injuries sustained therein. Every effort should be made to demolish the buildings as soon as possible after they are vacated.

WORK PERFORMED BY CONTRACTORS
VERSUS CITY PERSONNEL

There are certain respective benefits and liabilities in having demolition and site clearance activities carried out either by city personnel or by a demolition contractor. If the work to be performed is fairly extensive and the contractors have reasonable assurance of the continuity of the work, competitive bidding will generally result in lower costs than if the same works is performed by city personnel.

The contractor usually has the specialized experience and know-how to perform this type of work, and is able to plan the utilization of labor and equipment on the most economical basis. In addition, he generally has more knowledge of the techniques necessary to dispose of salvable items at the greatest profit. This potential source of profit may in some cases be the basis of a substantially lower bid on the part of the contractor.

If qualified city personnel and required equipment are available for the demolition or site clearance work, there could be some advantages in their utilization. City employees may tend to adhere more closely to the specifications, thus reducing or eliminating the need for separate inspection personnel. If properly staffed and programmed, the city employees could also be available for this work as needed, while performing other essential work between demolition jobs.

Demolition of structures is dangerous work which requires specialized knowledge and skills. Work improperly or carelessly performed could result in loss of life or damage to property with resultant liability. Although city personnel may be able to do satisfactorily certain site clearance work and the demolition of some smaller buildings, it is generally not prudent for them to undertake the demolition of larger structures, or to carry on such activities where remaining structures are closely adjacent to the buildings required to be razed. In any event, the LPA should weigh the respective benefits and liabilities before attempting to carry out demolition and site clearance activities with city personnel.

SCOPE AND PHASING OF DEMOLITION ACTIVITIES

There are no firm rules concerning the scope and phasing of demolition activities. Under certain conditions it may be desirable to advertise and award certain work singly or in small packages. This is especially true when there is no guaranty of the continuity of the work, or when it requires particular skill, such as the demolition of a large multistoried structure in an area with heavy traffic.

Award of the work in small packages may often present a greater opportunity for participation by small local contractors who may be incapable of handling a large job. The negative aspect of this approach is, as each new contract is awarded, it becomes necessary to reorient the new contractor to the requirements of the specifications and the intentions of the LPA concerning compliance therewith.

Normally the best price and greatest bidding competition can be obtained when there is assurance that a substantial number of buildings will be available for demolition upon award of the contract, and the LPA has acquired and/or has under option a substantial number of other buildings, together with the potential relocation resources, to assure a continuity in the release of buildings.

After the award of the contract, unless such continuity is maintained, the contractor may remove his equipment and manpower to another job, which could cause disruptions in scheduled disposal of property or utilization of less responsible subcontractors by the contractor.

Building Identification

In order to assure the demolition of the correct building, a means of identification should be established. The building address alone may not be satisfactory because there may be no address number on the building, and/or the demolition personnel may become confused with the streets and select the correct number on the wrong street for demolition. A safe method of identification, in addition to the address, is to assign a number to each building, paint that number, which agrees with the number shown on the release order, in a conspicuous manner on the front of the building, and/or attach a photograph of the building to the release order.

DEMOLITION AND SITE CLEARANCE FILES

Maintain the following files:
1. Specifications and contract forms.
2. Information regarding advertising.
3. Compilation of bids, and bid documents of unsuccessful bidders.
4. All information concerning successful bidder, including performance bond, bid bond, non-collusion affidavit, reference and credit checks, etc.
5. All information concerning subcontractors.
6. Release orders.
7. Daily inspection and progress reports.
8. Complaints.
9. Contractor's and subcontractor's payroll information.
10. Equal opportunity information including conferences with contractors and subcontractors relating thereto, employee complaints, interviews, etc.
11. Insurance coverage of contractors and subcontractors; keep note of all policy expiration dates.

12. Running record of status of each parcel and/or building listed in the demolition and site clearance documents, which include:
   a. Parcel and/or building identification and address.
   b. Date vacated by last occupant.
   c. Notice to utility companies or city to remove and/or discontinue utility service.
   d. Date building boarded up (if applicable).
   e. Date of release to contractor.
   f. Name of demolition firm.
   g. Date building exterminated.
   h. Date building demolition started.
   i. Date building demolition completed. Insurance company may require that dates of liability rate changes for each building be determined. Date may also be necessary in order to assure proper removal of structure from tax roll or tax credit. (Written notification of building removal should be given to assessor and/or other tax officials as necessary.)
   j. Date basement fill completed (if applicable).
   k. Date site grading completed.
   l. Comments.

13. Cross reference site clearance work done under same contract with site improvement work to applicable latter file. (Example: broken sidewalks removed prior to installation of new sidewalks. As this work is generally performed under a single contract, it would be a waste of time, effort, and space to duplicate the documentation in relation thereto in both files.)

NOTE:

If work is performed by city personnel (force account), items 2, 3, 4, 5, 9, 10, 11 would be eliminated. In lieu of item 9, required information would be kept of all costs and expenditures to the city. In item 1, specifications would be kept, but in lieu of contract documents required relative to a bid offering, supplemental agreements would be kept, such as for the rental of equipment or supply of fill dirt.

chapter 10

Project Improvements

7209.1, chaps. 1, 3, 4

The term *project improvements* covers the installation, construction, or reconstruction of public improvements within a project area which are necessary for carrying out the objectives of the urban renewal plan. As in demolition and site clearance, a project improvement either may be charged as Item I (project expense) or may be offered as Item II (non-cash, local grant-in-aid) activity (see 7209.1, chap. 1 for list of eligible and ineligible project improvements).

PREPARATION OF BID DOCUMENTS AND RELATED MATERIAL

7209.1, chap. 4, sec. 2

The LPA seldom has a professional engineer on its staff and so it is generally desirable to contract with an engineer for the preparation of the necessary bid documents and related material at the same time or immediately following the preparation of the demolition and site clearance documents. To make a contract with the same engineer for preparation of both sets of documents can result in a cost saving because many of the provisions of the bid documents for both types of work are the same or similar.

Once the basic format is prepared, it can be followed with minor changes for subsequent contracts. HUD will provide guide forms for the preparation of the necessary bid documents.

The preparation of the plans and specifications depends on the tim-

81

ing of the improvements, and whether they are to be installed under one contract or under several contracts. If it is contemplated that the work be done through several contracts, the plans and specifications for the first stage can usually be prepared in conjunction with the preparation of the basic bid documents and related material.

If site clearance work, such as the removal of old sidewalks prior to the installation of new sidewalks, is included in the contract, the bid prices of these items should be clearly separated from those for project improvements.

COMPLIANCE WITH CONTRACT DOCUMENTS

If the work is performed under contract, it should be ascertained that the contractor fully complies with the plans, specifications, and other applicable provisions of the contract. Most project improvement work should be subject to continuous inspection by a staff or city inspector, or a representative of the LPA engineering consultant so that strict adherence to the plans and specifications will be insured.

If unit prices are included in the bid, such as a specified price per cubic yards of concrete, then an accurate record should be kept by the inspector to substantiate the actual quantities delivered and put in place.

The inspector should also spot-check the contractor's conformance with prevailing wage determinations by interviews with workmen of the various trades; keep a record of the hours worked and be prepared to certify the correctness of the contractor's and subcontractor's payroll schedules submitted to the LPA; and check conformance with equal employment opportunity requirements.

WORK PERFORMED BY CONTRACTORS
VERSUS CITY PERSONNEL

Project improvements, with demolition and site clearance work, can be installed or constructed either by the city personnel or by a contractor. Under certain circumstances, or for those types of work where the city has the necessary experienced manpower and equipment, it might be more feasible for the work to be done by force account. Under other circumstances it might be more desirable for the work to be done under contract. In any event, the city should weigh the respective benefits and liabilities before attempting to carry out project improvement activities with city personnel.

Prior HUD concurrence in writing is required for a proposal to perform work by force account, when any portion is to be charged as an Item I project cost. Concurrence may be granted when the LPA has submitted convincing evidence that the performance of the work by force account rather than under private contract is advantageous or in accordance with local practice.

TIMING

Proper timing of project improvements can contribute substantially to the success of the project. In a rehabilitation section of a project, the performance of such work as the installation of sewers, water mains, new streets, curbs, and sidewalks is tangible evidence that the city is fulfilling its obligation to improve the area, just as the property owners are expected to do their part in improving their individual properties.

In a clearance area, demolition in a particular section should be completed. This will prevent damage to work already completed, such as new curbs or sidewalks. If such work is performed prior to the completion of demolition, extreme care to prevent such damage should be exercised by the demolition contractor. If damage is caused by the activities of the contractor, he should be held liable thereof.

In many instances, developers who purchased land prefer that some project improvements, such as the construction of sidewalks, be performed toward the completion of their development. In other cases, it may be essential that improvements, such as sewers, water lines, and streets, be installed prior to the commencement of construction by a redeveloper to provide access to the site of the development. Unfortunately, it is quite rare that project improvements can be phased so perfectly that all parties concerned are satisfied.

Close coordination between the various project activities and proper scheduling of the various activities greatly expedite the proper timing of project improvements.

PROJECT IMPROVEMENTS FILES

Maintain the following files:
1. Plans, specifications, and contract forms.
2. Information regarding advertising.
3. Compilation of bids and bid documents of unsuccessful bidders.
4. Information concerning successful bidder, including bid prices,

performance bond, bid bond, non-collusion affidavit, references, and credit checks, etc.

5. All information concerning subcontractors.
6. Notice to proceed.
7. Progress reports.
8. Complaints.
9. Contractors' and subcontractors' payroll information.
10. Equal opportunity information.
11. Insurance coverage; keep notice of policy expiration dates.

NOTE:

If work is performed by city personnel (force account), items 2, 3, 4, 5, 9, 10, and 11 would be eliminated. In lieu of item 9, a detailed record should be kept of all the costs and expenditures by the city. In item 1, specifications would be kept, but in lieu of contract documents required relative to bid offering, supplemental agreements are kept, such as for the rental of equipment or supply of fill dirt.

chapter 11

Land Marketing and Redevelopment

7214.1;

7384.1, chap. 6

Disposal of project land must be considered early in the project planning or NDP stage. Consideration should also be given to the objectives
of the community as they relate to the comprehensive plan, the needs of
the community both private and public, the fullest and best use of the
land, and its marketability. Information thereof can be obtained
through discussions with local realtors, builders, businessmen, public
officials, and the project planners. A Land Utilization and Marketability
Study (LUMS) or Economic and Market Analysis Study (EMAS) by a
competent firm of land economists should outline the best uses for the
land, such as its marketability, and make recommendations concerning
the size of the disposal parcels, and suggest the development of mar-
kets thereof. Reuse appraisers can also give valuable assistance and
advice concerning the sale of project land.

A lay person might think that by utilizing such a wide range of expert
advice and assistance, a successful land disposal program will automati-
cally be insured. Thousands of acres of unsold urban renewal land
throughout the country are stark reminders to the contrary.

SECURING DEVELOPERS

Except for projects located in large cities, metropolitan areas, or at
key locations, the best source of securing developers lies within the
community itself or its general environs. Existing industrial or business
firms may have a need for additional land to expand or relocate. Occu-

pants of property to be acquired may desire to relocate within the project area. Local residential builders may welcome the opportunity to obtain moderately priced land with all utilities and approved for various forms of HUD financing, in lieu of the high cost and effort of subdividing and developing a site for building.

Local interest can be stimulated by publicizing the project plans and progress through the local news media. Scale models, renderings, brochures, and other means can be utilized to stimulate interest. A list should be maintained of all interested and potentially interested parties who should be kept informed concerning the status of the project and the availability of sites suitable for their expressed purposes. This list is often the most valuable source of potential developers.

PHASING DISPOSITION

Property disposition can and should take place in most projects while property acquisition is still under way. This can be accomplished by the proper phasing of disposition activities, particularly in the disposal of small parcels.

The phasing of the disposition activities insures against the oversaturation of the land market at a given time, and provides for a more gradual absorption period. It also gives site occupants required to move by project activities the opportunity to relocate within the project area, and at the same time gives potential developers the opportunity to test the market on a small scale in order to determine the nature of the market demand.

TIMING

Timing is also very important. The offering of residential sites may be adversely affected if abutting sites still contain dilapidated buildings which are to be razed. The sale of a large industrial tract consisting of several parcels may be frustrated by selling the parcels off piecemeal. One or two of the smaller parcels may be sold, but such sales may preclude the sale of the balance to developers who desire only larger tracts.

DISPOSAL METHODS — LAND LEASING

There are various HUD approved methods of offering and disposing of project land. Land may also be leased to a developer on a long term basis. At the expiration of the lease, the property with the improvements thereon would revert back to the LPA.

A long term lease is a lease for a period of time, usually more than 40 years but in no event less than 25 years (see 7214.1, chap. 2, sec. 3 for information concerning the disposal of project land by long term lease).

The disposal of land for low or moderate income housing is subject to special statutory requirements and HUD adopted policies and procedures (see 7214.1, chap. 3).

The *Urban Renewal Handbook* contains detailed information concerning land disposal methods and procedures for offering land to private developers. The information generally does not recommend which method should be utilized in disposing of project land. This is usually a local determination which should be arrived at through a study of the various parcels in relation to the project objectives and local conditions. Within a particular project several methods may be utilized.

HUD has established five standard methods for offering land to private developers for redevelopment (see 7214.1, chap. 4, sec. 1 and 2). These methods are:

1. Fixed-price competition
2. Competition-negotiation combination
3. Sealed bids
4. Public auction
5. Predetermined prices for subdivision of small parcels

HUD regulations also permit a negotiated disposal for special redevelopers (see 7214.1, chap. 4, sec. 3). These include:

1. Sale for moderate income housing.
2. Sale for low income housing.
3. Sale of certain industrial and commercial land.
4. Disposal for public or non-profit institutional use.
5. Disposal for project improvements and easements for public utilities.
6. Sale for right-of-way for federal-aid highway.
7. Sale to the Federal Government.
8. Disposal to a private redeveloper for post office.
9. Sale or lease to a private redeveloper for whom all or most of the land has a special adaptability.
10. Early agreement on disposal to a private redeveloper.
11. Preference to project area owners or occupants.
12. Preference to an owner in or abutting project area.
13. Sale of small not separately usable parcel to an abutting property owner.
14. Exchange of land to adjust lot lines and/or minimize severance damage.

Whenever feasible, compatible with project objectives and authorized by state and local law, it is desirable to negotiate with and give preference to displaced project occupants.

STAFF RESPONSIBILITY

Because of the various methods by which project land may be offered for sale, and the various types of land-developers who may be involved in a project, there is no pat approach to the diverse situations which may arise. Generally it is the function of the LPA director, land disposition personnel, and, in a larger LPA, the public relations specialist, acting jointly, to stimulate interest in the land. The various alternative uses of a parcel of land permitted under the urban renewal plan should also be considered by the staff. The director should be prepared to make specific or various recommendations to the governing body of the LPA. Upon authorization of the governing body the staff will proceed with the necessary negotiations or take the required steps for a public offering.

Under certain circumstances, or in the disposal of a key parcel, it may be desirable for the potential developer or developers to meet with the governing body and make a presentation of their respective proposals. It may also be desirable, as in the case of a design competition, for the LPA to engage outside consultants to assist in making recommendations concerning proposed developments. Except for the legal work involved in the actual disposal, it is the responsibility of the LPA director or his staff representatives, working in conjunction with city inspection personnel, to follow the development from the award to the completion of the improvements. Upon the completion of the development in accordance with the approved plans, the LPA will issue a certificate of completion.

ROLE OF ATTORNEY

The work normally performed by the attorney relative to land disposition is as follows:

1. Prepare bid forms, disposal documents, including various deeds and contracts for the sale of land (based upon HUD guide forms), forms of resolutions for council approval, certificate of completion, etc.
2. Once the basic forms are prepared, either the person charged with the disposition activities prepares them for each individual trans-

action and then submits the various documents to the attorney for review prior to execution, or the necessary information is submitted to the attorney for him to complete the forms.
3. The actual closing may be handled either by LPA qualified personnel or the attorney.
4. If the closing is held by LPA personnel, then a duplicate or conformed copy of the executed disposition agreements and deeds should be submitted to the attorney as the basis of his opinion to be submitted to HUD.
5. If title insurance is utilized, a title insurance policy will then be given to the purchaser following the closing and filing of deed.

The many details involved from the acceptance of an offer or bid to the issuance of a certificate of completion makes it desirable that a close check be kept on the progress of each transaction (see Appendix 7, Checklist of Land Disposition Procedures).

CHRONOLOGY OF LAND MARKETING AND REDEVELOPMENT ACTIVITIES

1. Interview reuse appraisers and land marketing consultants and determine their respective qualifications.
2. Contract for necessary land use studies:
   a. If NDP, ordinarily one EMAS will be sufficient for an entire NDP area; however, each NDP urban renewal area within the NDP area may have to be separately analyzed. The EMAS for the entire area may be completed during the action year; however, if disposal of land is contemplated in a portion or portions, then provision should be made as soon as possible for receipt of reports covering those portions.
   b. If conventional project, LUMS is generally made early in the project planning stage.
3. If residential reuse is contemplated, consult with HUD concerning the suitability of the sites for such use.
4. If necessary, prepare parcel surveys, replats, and other engineering studies based upon land marketing study recommendations and/or other considerations.
5. Compile a list of property to be disposed of, based upon land marketing and engineering studies and surveys, if applicable, and other information available. The list should contain the parcel numbers, dimensions, square footage, proposed reuse, and legal

descriptions with spaces provided for subsequent reuse appraisal amounts, price established by LPA under proclaimer procedure, price submitted to HUD for concurrence, if required, and price eventually concurred in by HUD. Show priorities, if any.

6. Contract for reuse appraisals:

   a. If NDP and the land disposal are to take place in same action year as appraisals, then both appraisals should be made as soon as possible after accurate list of property with pertinent information is compiled.

   b. If conventional project, first reuse appraisals should be made in the project planning stage and the second appraisal should be made in the execution stage after acquisition and relocation have proceeded to a degree that the LPA can reasonably forecast when the land would be available for disposition.

7. Shortly after entering the execution stage of a conventional project, the LPA should develop a schedule of the necessary preparatory actions for submission to HUD.

8. Within the year prior to offering residential land for sale, the LPA should notify the HUD area or regional office of the contemplated disposal dates.

9. Land preparation prior to disposal: Following acquisition of the real estate, it may be necessary for the LPA to expedite certain actions. For example, if vacated streets, alleys, and other public rights-of-way are to be parts of the disposal parcel, then necessary actions should be taken to vacate same as soon as possible after acquisition of abutting property. If new streets or other public rights-of-way abutting the disposal parcel are to be dedicated, then these actions should also be taken. If new streets are involved, it may be necessary actually to construct the street improvements in order to provide access to the parcel.

10. Prepare bid forms and disposal documents, including the various deed and contract forms required. Submit to HUD for approval.

11. Analyze and reconcile the reuse appraisals.

12. Establish disposal price either by proclaimer procedure or with HUD concurrence, as applicable. About three months before the formal offering, the LPA should submit to HUD reuse appraisals, together with a request for concurrence on proposed disposal price, if the nature of the disposition does not permit the LPA to establish the disposal price under the proclaimer

procedure. If the LPA can establish the price under the proclaimer procedure, the appraisals shall not be submitted to HUD except in the following case. If the proposed disposal is for private redevelopment for residential uses, HUD will review the appraisals and related studies for mortgage insurance purposes. If satisfactory, HUD will approve the value attributed to the land for mortgage purposes and grant a reservation for the number of dwelling units it is willing to issue commitments to insure.

13. Offering land for sale. Details concerning methods of offering land for sale, and procedures after choosing the method selected should follow applicable provisions of the *Urban Renewal Handbook* 7214.1.
14. Resolution of governing body approving redeveloper, subject to approval of HUD.
15. Submit redeveloper's Statement for Public Disclosure to HUD for clearance before executing disposal agreement.
16. Publish public notice of proposed sale.
17. Execute disposal agreement.
18. Send opinion of LPA attorney concerning agreement to HUD.
19. Developer submits construction plans for approval by LPA.
20. Developer notified of plan approval.
21. Deed delivered to developer, upon receipt of payment.
22. Send opinion of LPA attorney concerning deed to HUD.
23. Order title insurance policy.
24. Deliver title insurance policy to developer.
25. Check construction progress.
26. Issue Certificate of Completion upon completion of improvements.
27. Return deposit (if held).

LAND MARKETING AND REDEVELOPMENT FILES

Maintain the following files:
1. LUMS, EMAS, and other applicable studies.
2. Reuse appraisals.
3. List of potential developers; nature of interest (commercial, industrial, specific parcels, dates of contracts, etc.).
4. Each land offering including, as applicable, the following:
   a. Approval by governing body of disposal method.
   b. Bid documents including advertisements, non-collusion af-

fidavits, statement of qualifications and financial responsibility, proposed agreement form, deed, etc.

    c. HUD approval of bid documents.
    d. Record of advertising.
    e. Bidders list and record of bids and/or record of negotiations.
    f. HUD approval of disposal prices and other related data (residential).

5. Maintain a separate file folder for each disposal parcel. Include in folder:

    a. If public bid, information with regard to bid; if negotiated, information concerning negotiations.
    b. Bidder's statement of Qualifications and Financial Responsibility, non-collusion affidavit, bid form as completed, proposed plans, etc. (If more than one parcel awarded to bidder, cross reference file to where foregoing documents are located, i.e., bid file or other parcel file.)
    c. Memo to governing body containing information concerning the bid or offer received, and recommendations thereon.
    d. Resolution of governing body containing the required findings and award to the developer or successful bidder.
    e. Submission of required documentation to HUD, together with request for concurrence in the sale, or proclaimer documentation.
    f. HUD approval (if required).
    g. Copy of disposition notice (advertisement in local newspaper or posted).
    h. Copy of disposition agreement.
    i. Copy of development plans.
    j. Copy of deed or indenture.
    k. Copy of Certificate of Completion.
    l. Title commitment and title policy (copy).
    m. Attorney opinions.

6. Maintain complete chronology of each disposal parcel on master sheet (see appendix 7 — Checklist of Land Disposition Procedures).

chapter 12

Rehabilitation

7210.1

In a federally assisted urban renewal program, rehabilitation is the type of renewal treatment which may be appropriate for the restoration of economic and social values of deteriorating areas that are basically sound and worth conserving, and in which existing buildings, public facilities, and improvements can be economically renewed to a long-term sound condition.

An entire project may be considered as a rehabilitation area, possibly with some spot clearance, or parts of a project may be clearance areas and parts, rehabilitation areas. Although rehabilitation may include residential, non-residential, or mixed use property, different sets of standards are applicable to residential and non-residential property.

PROPERTY REHABILITATION STANDARDS

7210.1, chap. 1, sec. 5

The attainment of the rehabilitation objectives of the project should be in conformance with the Property Rehabilitation Standards (PRS) established for the particular project. The PRS for residential property generally requires compliance with the housing code and other applicable codes of the community, together with the above-code or more stringent standards (if any) contained in the urban renewal plan. Above-code provisions are required to be inserted in the urban renewal plan when the existing codes are not adequate to assure the restoration to a sound condition of properties in the rehabilitation area which will meet

HUD's established criteria. The minimum criteria are contained in the HUD publication, PG-50, *Rehabilitation Guide for Residential Properties*.

The PRS for non-residential property are usually less exacting and less clearly delineated, but they are spelled out in general terms in the urban renewal plan.

The above-code standards to be inserted in the urban renewal plan should be developed through consultation with HUD staff. Approval of the project's PRS will assure the availability of HUD loans and grants and mortgage insurance financing for rehabilitation properties located in the project area.

At the time of final project audit, PRS shall have been accomplished on at least 75 percent of the properties which have been retained, and code standards shall have been attained on at least 95 percent of the properties retained.

QUALIFICATIONS OF THE REHABILITATION SPECIALIST

As in other phases of urban renewal, one of the major problems of the administrator is the selection of the best qualified person or persons to fit the particular job.

The qualifications of the rehabilitation specialist are somewhat similar to those of the building inspector in that both should have some experience in building materials, methods, and techniques. As the building inspector's work primarily involves the inspection of new buildings, or the alteration of existing buildings following the issuance of a building or alteration permit, his work is of a more specialized nature, with emphasis on technical know-how. His services, together with those of the electrical, plumbing, and other city inspectors, are utilized as applicable in the rehabilitation of project property, following the issuance of a permit.

The inspection work of the rehabilitation specialist is more generalized in nature, but in effect requires a selling ability plus a flair for positive human relations. In many communities the rehabilitation specialist is also directly involved in the financing of property improvements by arranging federal loans and grants, and recommending conventional sources of loans when applicable.

Experience in the building trades, real estate, property management or maintenance, or certain phases of insurance may provide an excellent background for the rehabilitation specialist. He should be intelligent, capable of understanding and interpreting the various codes, ordinances, and standards contained in the urban renewal plan. He should have a basic knowledge or familiarity with property improvement financing and, most importantly, be responsive to the public.

In addition to his other duties, the rehabilitation specialist acts as a liaison between the owners of property remaining in the project area and the other project and public officials, a position similar to that the relocation specialist performs with displacees. A great deal of the project's success depends on the manner in which the rehabilitation specialist carries out his assigned functions; therefore, his selection should be made with care.

OBTAINING COOPERATION OF PROPERTY OWNERS

The rehabilitation goals of a project should be explained to the property owners, together with the economic and social benefits that can accrue to them through the attainment of these goals.

Rehabilitation should be characterized as a cooperative venture between the property owners and the city. The city is to provide certain public improvements to enhance the area at no cost to the property owners and, at the same time, assist the individual owner in counseling him concerning property improvement and, if necessary, in financing the required improvements through loans and/or grants.

The rehabilitation specialist should use the "soft sell" approach, but he should not hesitate to be firm or recommend affirmative action by the LPA when necessary. In no event should he act in an overbearing or dictatorial manner. If a particular owner or owners refuse to permit the inspection, or refuse to eliminate certain defects in their property, the matter should be reported to the director. Upon authorization of the governing body, legal action may be instituted against the owner or the property placed on the acquisition list if provision therefore is contained in the urban renewal plan.

Although the upgrading of deteriorating property should be the prime concern of the rehabilitation specialist, he should not ignore the potential of further improvements to properties which fully meet the project requirements at the inception of the program. In many projects, some of the most dramatic improvements are made by the owners of such properties. They often include persons who have the financial ability to make such improvements and who have demonstrated the desire for above average maintenance of their property.

Property improvement is contagious and the more people who can be encouraged to upgrade their facilities in a given block, the greater the potential that their neighbors will do likewise.

NON-COMPLIANCE OF PROPERTY OWNERS

In rehabilitation, primary reliance is placed on the cooperation of the property owner in order to achieve compliance with the project's rehabilitation objectives. Although the LPA can generally seek redress against code violators in the courts, it cannot take any legal action against owners who fail to meet the above-code requirements.

It is desirable to provide in the urban renewal plan for the acquisition of properties slated for rehabilitation, when the owner thereof is either unwilling or unable to rehabilitate his property. It is therefore important that a statement of the special conditions be incorporated in the urban renewal plan under which properties not conforming to the PRS and objectives of the urban renewal plan may be acquired (see 7210.1, chap. 1, sec. 5, appendix 1 for suggested form of statement).

Even if the acquisition of such properties is not comtemplated in the project planning stage, the fact that provision therefore is made in the urban renewal plan often provides the LPA with the leverage necessary to obtain compliance.

RECOGNITION OF OWNER COMPLIANCE

Each owner of property who complies with or exceeds the project objectives should be given some form of recognition. This may take the form of a decal to apply on a window, indicating this attainment, and/ or a certificate or letter from the mayor, city manager, or urban renewal director complimenting the owner, or some other form of recognition.

Outstanding examples of property rehabilitation may deserve a plaque or some similar form of recognition. This may be awarded by the mayor at a meeting of the city council, or at a meeting of the citizen's organization for the project. Presentations of this nature should be well publicized in the newspapers and other public information media.

INSPECTION OF PROPERTIES

The first complete inspection of each parcel will generally take place during the project planning period or in the NDP first action year. If the community is undertaking its first program, this inspection will generally be made by the city building department or by consultants or others on a contract basis. If the city has had a previous project involving rehabilitation and conservation, a staff rehabilitation specialist may make this initial inspection. If the project does not have such a specialist on its staff, it is of utmost importance that one be hired soon enough to become familiar with the project requirements and procedures. This will eliminate delays in carrying out rehabilitation activities when the LPA enters the project execution or NDP action stages.

If the rehabilitation specialist has not made the previous inspections, he should make a complete inspection of each property upon commencement of rehabilitation activities. If he did make the previous inspections, he should again view the property to determine if any improvements were made, or whether any further deterioration has taken place since the prior inspection.

INSPECTION FOLLOW-UP

The inspection of each property should be followed by a written report to the owner outlining the work required to be done, if any. The rehabilitation specialist should also attempt to obtain a commitment from the owner as to when the work will be performed. He should offer to assist in the evaluation of contractor's plans, proposals, and specifications. If applicable, he may offer the services of an architect retained by the LPA to make recommendations for structural changes or improvements.

The rehabilitation specialist should schedule periodic visits to the various properties to determine what improvements, if any, were made since his previous visit, and the nature and cost thereof. He should maintain a record of each visit to each property and also a record of each contact with the owner or tenant, together with a brief summary of the discussions.

Whenever feasible, information concerning the owner's financial status should be obtained in order to determine the possible eligibility for a rehabilitation grant. The owners should also be advised concerning the availability of rehabilitation loans.

EFFECT OF SPOT CLEARANCE ON REHABILITATION

Spot clearance of dilapidated property generally has a positive effect in generating rehabilitation activity. If the adjacent remaining property is situated on a small lot, whenever feasible the owner or owners of the structures remaining should be approached concerning their interest in purchasing all or part of the adjacent lot in order to enhance their property and the neighborhood. This is also an excellent means of disposing of lots that are below the project's minimum size requirements for development.

In any event, dilapidated structures should be acquired and razed as soon as possible in order to eliminate their blighting effect. If the land is not sold to adjacent property owners, it should be sold for development without undue delay. The construction of new buildings among older buildings has a tremendous effect in upgrading a neighborhood and stimulating improvements to the older buildings.

REHABILITATION FILES

Maintain the following files and records:
1. Case file: A separate file folder should be maintained for each structure or group of structures under the same ownership remaining in the project area on a particular parcel which are placed on the rehabilitation work load.

    Each case file folder should contain the following:
    a. Parcel number
    b. Name and address of owner
    c. Name and address of each tenant and/or location, i.e., apartment number, office number.
    d. Type of structure or structures, i.e., single family, residential, commercial, etc.
    e. Use or various uses therein (if non-conforming use per zoning ordinance, specify non-conformance)
    f. Photographs of all structures (before and after)
    g. Inspection reports
    h. Correspondence concerning parcel
    i. Information concerning any federal loan and/or grants for parcel
    j. List of all improvements made: dates, cost
    k. Record of discussions with owner or others.
    l. Other applicable information
    All cases having the same or similar status should be grouped together and separated from cases in a different status. The various groups should be divided and identified by file dividers. The various classifications should include the following:

(a) Property upon which no rehabilitation work is started
(b) Property in the process of being rehabilitated
(c) Property in which completed rehabilitation meets code standards
(d) Property in which completed rehabilitation meets above-code to project standards (PRS)
(e) Further improvements to property which met PRS at inception of execution or NDP activities

As the status of each property changes, the file folder should be removed from the prior grouping and placed in the new grouping. No individual file folder should be taken out of the project office.

2. Inspection records of all property to be acquired
3. Inspection records of all property that met PRS at inception of execution activities and are not to be acquired. If further improvements are made or contemplated for any of these properties, the inspection record of each such property should be placed in a separate file folder together with any other data concerning the particular parcel, and filed with other such parcels per paragraph 1. (e) above.
4. Card file for rehabilitation specialist's field use. (Card should contain brief summary of applicable data with space for field notes concerning meetings with owners or other parties interested in property, improvements made, cost thereof, etc. Basic information to be transcribed to file folder upon return to office.)
5. List of pending and completed loans and grants showing:
   a. Name of owner
   b. Parcel number
   c. Address of property
   d. Status of loan and/or grant application
   e. Approved amount of loan and/or grant
   f. Various stages of pending applications
   g. Status of improvements
   h. Name and address of contractor
   i. Dates of payments made
   j. Date work completed
   k. Checklist of subcontractors and dates waiver of claims or releases received
6. Copy of applicable reports to HUD
7. Forms, form letters, etc.

8. Listing of various contractors
9. Product information files classified by products, i.e., storm doors, sidings, kitchen cabinets, hot water heaters, etc., and/or a library of same

chapter 13

Legal Matters

SCOPE OF LEGAL SERVICES—LEGAL FEES

Almost every aspect of urban renewal involves some legal participation, interpretation, or opinion. In most communities the services of legal counsel in urban renewal are generally casual rather than continuous. Therefore very few communities need a full time attorney on their staffs and the services of legal counsel should be engaged on a contract basis. The compensation and scope of services would vary, depending on the experience of the administrator and other staff employees, and the nature of work to be performed by the attorney. An experienced real estate man handling the acquisition and disposition of property functions, for example, may be thoroughly capable of handling many of the technical aspects of these functions by following the basic format of the instruments drafted by the attorney, including the preparation of the required documents for a particular transaction, the preparation of closing statement, and the actual closing. On the other hand, it may be more prudent for the project attorney to handle all or part of these activities.

For general consultative, minor litigation and various types of legal services the attorney is usually retained on an hourly basis with the fee based upon the local bar association approved schedule of minimum fees or, if none, prevailing fees in the community. The contract with the attorney normally includes in the approved fee schedule all his overhead costs, but not out-of-pocket expenses such as recording fees, for which he would be entitled to reimbursement. The contract may also stipulate a per diem amount for services performed a full day such as extensive litigation or travel to the regional offices of HUD for necessary conferences regarding project activities. He would also be reimbursed for such out-of-town travel expenses.

The nature of the attorney's participation in land acquisition and disposition activities will determine if a fee should be stipulated for such transactions. The amount of the fee would be arrived at by mutual agreement between the attorney and the LPA after the scope of the attorney's services is agreed upon. The fee could be set on an hourly basis; on a set amount for each closing; on a percentage value of the property acquired or sold; or such other equitable basis agreed upon and provided for in the contract for legal services.

In addition to the usual advice and necessary legal opinions, the attorney may be called upon to perform many legal services. These may include preparation and/or review of contracts and other legal documents, preparation of resolutions to be adopted by the local governing body, rezoning of project land, street and alley vacations, dedication of project land for public purposes, evictions and/or court actions for the collection of delinquent rent accounts, etc.

The attorney's bill to the LPA should detail the specific nature of each service performed, and if rendered upon an hourly basis, the time should be broken down to the nearest quarter hour for compensation purposes.

LITIGATION

Contracts involving litigation, other than the minor type of court actions of the nature shown above, must receive prior HUD approval. These generally include actions attacking the validity of the project or project activities, actions for damages, actions raising constitutional issues, etc. (see 7217.1, chap. 2, relative to Contracts for Professional and Technical Services). The LPA shall promptly report to HUD any pending or threatened litigation relating to an urban renewal project activity (see 7205.1, chap. 3, for requirements of reporting such litigation).

SPECIAL LEGAL KNOWLEDGE REQUIRED

In many respects, the legal aspects of an urban renewal program are specialized in nature, and require a knowledge of federal and state laws relating thereto; a knowledge of HUD regulations, requirements, and procedures; as well as other related activities. A knowledgeable legal counsel can contribute greatly to the success of a project. However, his acquiring a basic knowledge of urban renewal matters should not be at the expense of the project. This does not preclude research into certain aspects of the applicable laws or regulations in order to render an opinion or determination, for which he is entitled to compensation.

LIMITATIONS OF ATTORNEY'S FUNCTION

It is not the function of the project attorney to render an opinion in a purely administrative matter, nor should the administrator call on the attorney to render other than legal services or services not included in the scope of his contract. The relation with the attorney should be one of mutual confidence, but this does not preclude the administrator or the governing body of the LPA from questioning certan of his recommendations or determinations. The fact that the attorney advised improperly in a certain matter, or submitted a statement for services performed that was not properly detailed or was not within the scope of the contract, does not excuse the error or omission and could be the basis of an audit finding by HUD.

LEGAL FILES

Legal papers relating to specific parcels should generally be contained among the records of the parcel such as those relating to acquisition, disposition, or condemnation. Legal papers relating to matters such as project applications and opinions relating thereto should generally be contained with the records of such subjects. Legal papers concerning actions, proceedings, or other matters, which generally affect the project as a whole or segments of the project area which are not included in the foregoing, should be contained in separate legal files. These would include the following:

1. Litigation: File each action separately. The LPA should keep a copy of all pleadings and other related documentation in its files, in addition to those maintained by the attorney. Condemnation actions may be filed under this classification until completion, after which time all papers relating thereto should be placed in the applicable acquisition parcel folder.
2. Zoning changes
3. Street and alley vacations
4. Dedications of land for public purposes
5. Replats
6. Cooperation agreements with other public bodies

7. Agreements with public utility companies
8. Easements received, granted, or eliminated
9. Removal of deed restrictions involving several parcels or an entire subdivision
10. Miscellaneous

chapter 14

Project Financing

7215.1

7385.1

The administration of an urban renewal project involves many complex financing transactions. These include private financing with a federal guarantee of payment, federal loans and grants, financing the local share of project costs through a bond issue or other means, investment of project funds, and the utilization of monies earned from the sale of acquired real estate.

The *Urban Renewal Handbook* details information about developing the financing plan, survey and planning funds, federal grants, borrowing funds to meet project costs, investment of excess cash, and local grants-in-aid. The purpose of this chapter is not to duplicate information contained in the *Urban Renewal Handbook* but to highlight certain areas in which prudent attention to financial details can substantially reduce ultimate project costs.

PRIVATE FINANCING

7215.1, chap. 4, sec. 2

Interest from Federal Government notes and bonds is taxable, but interest from municipal notes and bonds is not, therefore, banks and other moneylenders will generally pay a lower rate of interest for such municipal issues. This is especially true in urban renewal projects where private short-term loans are guaranteed and secured by the United States Government. In order to reduce interest charges it is generally advisable that the LPA finance project activities through private financing as soon as possible. The HUD regional offices strongly encourage this means of project financing, and are most helpful in assisting in the details.

When borrowing on the open market through federally secured loans, the loan period is generally from six to twelve months. It is usually desirable that the LPA borrow such funds for the longest period possible because longer term borrowing reduces the administrative costs resulting from borrowings of shorter term notes. Through the investment of money received and not needed for immediate project activities in such securities as United States treasury bills, at a generally higher interest return than the interest paid for private financing, the LPA will earn a profit on the borrowed money. This profit will reduce project costs.

DIRECT FEDERAL LOANS

7215.1, chap. 2, sec. 1; chap. 4, sec. 1

When private financing is not feasible, a direct federal loan may be necessary. This means of financing may be necessary when a project enters the execution stage and there will not be sufficient time for completion of the private financing transaction before the funds are needed; when a project is close to completion; or when private financing is not possible or feasible due to pending litigation or other reasons.

The government will also advance funds to cover necessary survey and planning activities in preparation of an urban renewal project, pursuant to the execution of a Contract for Planning Advance between the LPA and the government. In certain instances an LPA may finance survey and planning activities with its own funds.

PROGRESS PAYMENTS; ACCOUNT TRANSFERS

7215.1, chap. 3, sec. 1-4; chap. 4, sec. 4

Project interest charges can also be reduced through timely requisition of progress payments of federal grants, and through the transfer of funds from Project Temporary Loan Repayment Fund to Project Expenditure Account. Progress payments are payable at various stages of project activity if certain conditions are met and if the LPA is making satisfactory progress in the provision of local grants-in-aid. These are in the form of Capital Grant Progress Payments, Relocation Grant Payments, and Rehabilitation Grant Payments.

These payments are normally applied to reduce outstanding direct

temporary loans or any other amount due HUD in connection with the
project, and if no such loans are outstanding, it will generally be re-
mitted to the LPA for deposit in the Temporary Loan Repayment Fund,
and usually utilized as a partial payment of private notes at maturity.
Utilizing grant payments in this manner reduces interest charges on existing or future borrowings.

Transferring funds from the Project Temporary Loan Repayment
Fund to the Project Expenditures Account will generally alleviate the
necessity of borrowing an equivalent amount of money with the resulting saving of interest charges.

Normally all monies received by the LPA through federal and private
loans are deposited in the Project Expenditures Account during the
project execution stage. All monies received from the sale of real estate
or federal progress payments are deposited in the Project Temporary
Loan Repayment Fund. Project expenses are paid from the Expenditures Account. No such payments can be made from the Loan Repayment Fund nor may transfers of funds be made from the latter to the
Expenditures Account except by written consent of the HUD regional
office, upon application (Form H-6205 — Request for Consent to Transfer Funds). Such request will generally be granted if justification is
shown that the transfer is requested to avoid or reduce the cost of borrowing from other sources.

Federal grants are payable to the LPA in the following amounts:

a. Progress Payments

   (1) Capital grant payment: Periodic payments up to 75 percent
       of the approved estimate of grant payable

   (2) Relocation grant payment: Periodic reimbursement in full for
       properly made relocation payments

   (3) Rehabilitation grant payment: Periodic reimbursement in full
       for properly made rehabilitation grants

b. Other grant payments

   (1) Major completion grant payment: When project is substan-
       tially completed, including capital grant progress payments,
       it can equal 95 percent of approved estimate of grant pay-
       able.

   (2) Final capital grant payment: The final payment made at the
       time of financial settlement at completion of the project.
       This covers the remainder of the capital grant payable.

A financial settlement for a NDP shall be initiated within 30 days of
the close of the action year.

LOCAL GRANTS-IN-AID

7216.1; 7386.1; 7385.1, chap. 2, sec. 1

The required local share of a project cost must be contributed in the form of grants-in-aid. Local grants-in-aid consist of cash payments, land donations, and credits for certain non-federal expenditures for supporting facilities, project improvements, and activities that serve and benefit the urban renewal project.

Cash grants-in-aid shall generally be paid into the project accounts not later than the date on which the LPA is expected to become eligible for the first project capital grant progress payment or for a NDP within nine months after the beginning of the action year. Once the cash grants-in-aid are paid into the project accounts, there is no further concern therewith except in conformance with the normal accounting practices.

On the other hand, the provision of local non-cash grants-in-aid requires detailed record keeping, proper timing, and knowledge and attention to HUD requirements concerning eligibility. Close attention to these factors could often result in an excess of non-cash credits for a particular project which can later be used as pooling credits toward the local share of another project. Failure to pay attention to HUD requirements could result in a deficiency of non-cash credits, thus requiring that the local community provide additional cash to meet its share of the project obligations.

FINANCING FILES

The following files should be maintained for each transaction:
1. Direct federal loans (see 7215.1, chap. 4, sec. 1, for required information and documentation).
2. Federally secured private financing: Private financing arrangements are worked out jointly by the LPA and HUD regional office. The regional office will spell out the actions necessary on the local level, and the timing necessary for each private financing transaction (see 7215.1, chap. 4, sec. 2, for required information and documentation).
3. Local financing: Keep all relevant information and documentation for each urban renewal bond issue, and sources of project financing not included in items 1 and 2 above.
4. Investment of excess cash: resolution authorizing investment;

agreement with bank; record of each investment together with purchase and maturity date and copies of safekeeping receipts.

5. Transfers of project funds: All pending and approved HUD required forms.
6. Federal grants: Copies of all HUD required documentation. For list of required documentation for various types of grants, see 7215.1, chap. 3, sec. 4.
7. Local grants-in-aid (see 7216.1):

   Cash — Keep detailed records concerning cash grants-in-aid received and deposited to the project accounts.

   Non-cash — Detailed records should include the following:
   a. Land donations. Include dates, basis of values, etc.
   b. Accurate, up-to-date records of all non-cash credits proposed, underway, and completed.
   c. If work done by bid, keep tabulation of bids, etc.
   d. As improvements are completed, get as-built drawings, breakdown of final costs including construction, engineering, inspection, etc. Record dates of start and completion of work. Detail nature of work and, if applicable, unit cost prices, i.e., if work involves the reconstruction of a street, show (X) sq. yds. pavement removal, (Y) linear feet curb removal, (Z) sq. yds. new pavement, etc.
   e. Keep copies of form H-6202 (Certificate of Cost of Non-cash Grant-in-aid) submitted to HUD, copies of HUD approved forms, and all related documentation.
   f. If work done by force account such as city personnel, keep accurate time records of each person engaged in the work for which the credit is claimed, equipment used, basis of equipment charges, etc. Prorate to job the cost of equipment insurance, workman's compensation, and labor fringe benefits.

chapter 15

Accounting

The *Urban Renewal Handbook* prescribes the manner and means of keeping the books and records of account required for an urban renewal project. HUD will also assist the LPA in setting up the proper books of account.

State laws and/or the nature of the LPA organization, and/or the nature of local ordinances, customs, or desires may determine which personnel, if any, other than LPA staff, shall perform certain related activities. These may include check writing, approval and processing of claims payable, time keeping, calculation of payroll deductions, bank deposits, and even the keeping of separate books to conform with the system maintained for other city departments, in addition to those kept by LPA.

In view of the diversity of related activities which may be performed outside of the scope of LPA authority, and which vary from community to community, it would be difficult if not impossible to comment on each possible variation. Since LPA must maintain its books and records of account in conformance with HUD requirements, very often the public officials charged with such responsibility for the community as a whole may view such activities by the LPA with resentment or as an infringement upon their area of responsibility. Consequently, the establishment of good personal relationships and cooperation with such persons should be top priority.

CHECKS AND DEPOSITS

No matter who is authorized to write checks, no check should be drawn against any project account unless the statement or invoice for which the check is drawn is first approved by the urban renewal director or his duly authorized representative. Before any money is paid pursuant to a contract, the claim or statement should be reviewed by checking the provisions of the contract and conformance therewith, and by determining whether there is an adequate unpaid balance of the contract remaining to satisfy the claim. These reviews or determinations may be made by the bookkeeper before presenting the claims, invoices, or statements to the director for his approval.

The contract or a copy thereof should be readily accessible to the bookkeeper. A contract ledger should also be maintained, together with a record of all payments made.

Copies of all checks issued should be attached to the statement or invoice, or a copy thereof, and filed by project account. Copies of all bank deposit slips, Federal Reserve Bank safekeeping receipts or other evidence of invested project funds, receipts for funds delivered to other public officials for safekeeping or deposit, and petty cash vouchers should be kept.

THE BOOKKEEPER

A competent bookkeeper is a valuable asset to an urban renewal staff. A larger agency may employ a controller to supervise the bookkeeping operations. Experience and/or education in the basic principles of accounting are desirable qualifications of both. HUD provides detailed requirements on establishing and maintaining project books of account and related records, in accordance with acceptable accounting practices. The HUD prescribed requirements should be followed diligently even if they are not consistent with the basic system utilized by the community, or a type system with which the bookkeeper had prior familiarity. Failure to maintain books of account and related records could result in an audit finding by HUD auditors. A competent bookkeeper cannot be presumed to have a knowledge of all aspects of urban renewal, consequently she should be encouraged to confer with the administrator concerning the proper account classification for certain moneys disbursed or payments received. Depending on the size and scope of the local program, the bookkeeping services may be performed by a part-time bookkeeper, or by a person who performs other staff functions.

Under certain circumstances or for a very small LPA, it might be prudent to contract for bookkeeping services. If this is done, the cost thereof should be commensurate with a staff bookkeeper rather than with a certified public accountant. In order to eliminate the potential of an audit finding concerning the cost of such services, it is advisable to obtain HUD approval prior to entering into a contract for bookkeeping services.

As HUD periodically audits the LPA books and records of account, it is not normally necessary for the LPA to have an independent audit, and in fact such audit may not be an allowable project cost.

BOOKS AND RECORDS OF ACCOUNT

Separate books of account shall be maintained for each urban renewal project, feasibility survey, or general neighborhood renewal plan. Books of account and supporting documents shall be identified with the project or activity number and shall be established with the first transaction.

The required books of account are:
General Ledger
Subsidiary Cost Ledger
Cash Recipts Journal
Cash Disbursements Journal
General Journal (or Journal Vouchers)

The *Urban Renewal Handbook* (7221.1) provides detailed information on establishing and maintaining the LPA books of account and related records.

ACCOUNTS AND RELATED RECORDS FILES

(In addition to Books of Account)

Files of the following documents should be maintained:
1. Copies of all contracts (if not otherwise readily available to bookkeeper)
2. Contract ledger showing total contract amount with record of all payments made thereunder
3. Purchase orders together with all receiving and inspection reports

4. Invoices — paid when supported by proper documentation such as purchase orders or contracts

5. Payroll Records, including time and attendance records, leave records, payroll withholdings, and breakdown of employee time (if applicable). The latter should be kept on a pay period basis if LPA personnel are engaged in other activities in addition to project activities and/or if services are divided between more than one urban renewal project

6. Travel expense vouchers

7. Copies of check vouchers

8. Petty cash fund vouchers

9. Bank reconciliation with bank statement and cancelled checks. If same is received and kept by city treasurer or other public official, then keep copy of official's monthly report showing balance

10. Copies of Report of Budgetary Status — Form HUD-6250 as submitted to HUD semiannually

11. Copies of monthly operating summary showing budgetary status (for internal budgetary control)

12. Copies of Project Balance Sheet — Form HUD-6251 as submitted to HUD semiannually

13. Copies of bank deposit slips and/or receipts of moneys received by city treasurer or other public official who may be charged with depositing same in bank

14. Information and documentation relative to investment of project funds including investment dates and amounts and maturity dates and values

15. Miscellaneous related documentation

chapter 16

Citizen Participation

7387.1

7100.1

Citizen involvement in urban renewal is generally a basic ingredient of a successful program. Citizen participation and involvement may take many forms. These may include a community action committee of leading citizens promoting a project or the chamber of commerce, labor organizations, and service clubs endorsing the project plans and proposals or project area residents participating in the project activities.

It is a HUD requirement that citizens have the opportunity to participate in policies and programs that affect their welfare. The Workable Program requires clear evidence that the community provides opportunities for citizens, including those who are poor and the members of minority groups, to participate in urban renewal and related programs. The community is also expected, during each certification period, to show any progress made to achieve an adequate and effective degree of citizen involvement.

Unlike previous requirements, HUD no longer mandates the form that citizen participation must take in order to meet Workable Program requirements. The choice of mechanism depends upon the needs of the particular community and the structure of the local government. The Workable Program requires "continuing effort on the part of the community to improve and expand the opportunities for creative forms of participation and collaboration that both ensure representation by the poor and minority groups as well as enable government to take effective, purposeful, and expert action to deal with the problems and needs facing the community."

In addition to Workable Program requirements, it is HUD policy that during the preparation of the Urban Renewal Plan, the LPA should consult with residents of each proposed urban renewal area involving residential rehabilitation with respect to proposed boundaries and activities to take place within the area.

After selection of an urban renewal area involving residential rehabilitation, a Project Area Committee (PAC) should be established in cooperation with local residents and groups to participate in the planning and execution of activities within the area. The PAC should be composed of representatives of a fair cross section of residents of the area.

Citizen involvement in urban renewal may often have an adverse effect upon the program. Although much of the involvement may be positive and greatly benefit the program, it may often be of a negative and/or a self-serving nature. Some of the most actively involved groups and individuals may be bitterly opposed to the concept of urban renewal, may oppose particular aspects of the plans, or may object to proposed plans due to the effect upon them individually or collectively.

It is the function of the LPA director, acting in concert with the political and civic leaders of the community and project areas, to motivate the community toward proper action. The director should remain openminded toward recommendations concerning project proposals by sincerely interested citizens. On the other hand, changes in project proposals that would tend to frustrate the project objectives to the detriment of the community should be vigorously opposed.

The director or a duly designated representative should act as liaison between the LPA and the various citizen committees and coordinate, to the extent feasible, their recommendations with those of the project planners and technicians.

CITIZEN PARTICIPATION FILES

Citizen participation activities and organizational data relative to a particular project should be kept in the project files. Similar activities and organizational data which is community wide and/or not applicable to a particular project should be kept in the general files.

Maintain the following files as applicable:

1. Community-wide citizens' action committee
   a. Membership list
   b. Minutes of meetings

    c. Committee studies, reports, and recommendations
    d. Record of conferences with committee members, subcommittees, or study groups
2. Project area committees
    a. Membership list
    b. Minutes of meetings
    c. Committee studies, reports and recommendations
    d. Record of conferences with committee members, subcommittees, or study groups
3. Plans and proposals of committee technical advisors
4. Data concerning significant contributions or actions by other community or project area citizen organizations
5. Miscellaneous

chapter 17

Files and Record Keeping

The files and records of an urban renewal agency should be kept in an orderly, accessible manner. In addition to the project records and data, the files of the LPA normally contain a large amount of information and documentation not directly part of a particular project, e.g., city codes and ordinances, planning reports, state and federal laws, census data, various brochures, etc.

PROPOSED FILING SYSTEMS

Appendix 1 contains a recommended type of filing system for the LPA. Many LPAs are charged with the responsibility of administering other federally assisted programs in addition to urban renewal, such as Urban Beautification, Concentrated Code Enforcement, or Low Rent Public Housing.

The proposed filing system shown in Appendix 1 is in accordance with the following format for the major categories:

 100 Administration
 200 Community Planning
 300 Project Mich. R-47
 400 Project Mich. R-84
 500 Project Mich. R-102
 600 ⎫ Open for future
 700 ⎬ urban renewal or
 800 ⎭ other type projects
 900 General

If the LPA has jurisdiction over a large variety of programs, it can utilize the same format modified in the following manner:

                    100 Administration
                    200 Community Planning
    Mich. R-47 -300 Urban Renewal Projects
    Mich. R-84 -300 Urban Renewal Projects
    Mich. R-102-300 Urban Renewal Projects
    Mich. 51-1 -400 Housing Projects
    Mich. 51-2 -400 Housing Projects
    Mich. B-7 -500 Urban Beautification Projects
                    600 Code Enforcement Projects
                    700 Community Renewal Program
                    800 General Neighborhood Renewal Program
                    900 General

The above arrangement merely suggests the types of modifications possible within the framework of the recommended system.

PROJECT FILES

Project files and records should be organized and maintained in accordance with the following major classifications:
    LPA Administration
    Project Planning
    Real Estate Acquisition
    Property Management
    Relocation
    Demolition and Site Clearance
    Project Improvements
    Land Marketing and Disposition
    Rehabilitation
    Legal
    Project Financing
    Accounting
    Citizen Participation
    Miscellaneous
The files and records of each project should be maintained separately and not combined with the files of another project. The HUD project number should be shown on the tab of each file folder.

CORRESPONDENCE RECORDS

The maintenance of a good, readily accessible record of communications is a basic ingredient of proper record keeping. This should include the following:

1. A continuous record of all correspondence and memos of important phone calls (brief summary) to and from HUD should be maintained in Acco or similar binder by date (latest on top)
2. A continuous record of all other outside correspondence
3. A continuous record of all internal correspondence and memos to and from mayor, city manager, city council, other department heads, etc.

Extra copies of all correspondence should be put in the applicable file (e.g., letter to HUD with regard to a budget revision should go in the applicable budget file folder, in addition to the copy inserted in the HUD correspondence binder).

If the LPA administers several projects and/or several types of programs, the correspondence records may be maintained by project, such as separate continuous records for each project, as shown above, or they may be maintained on a program basis, with a consolidated continuous record for all urban renewal projects, one for all low rent housing projects and one for urban beautification projects, etc.

FORM FILES

The LPA should maintain a supply of all the forms commonly used in carrying out an urban renewal program. HUD forms should be requested form the regional office. Requests should be limited to a six month's supply and, in order to facilitate handling, should be the only subject of the correspondence (see list of Urban Renewal Forms — 7200.1, chap. 1, appendix 1; also see list of Neighborhood Development Forms — appendix 1 following Foreword of NDP *Handbook*).

Many HUD forms are guide forms for use by the LPA in preparation of its own forms. As the LPA will generally prepare many additional forms e.g., inspection reports, deeds, options, etc., it is desirable that a number be assigned to each locally prepared form and that a list of all such forms be kept.

A supply of each form should be kept in a file folder and filed in numerical order. All locally prepared forms should be dated in the same manner as HUD forms. Obsolete forms should be removed from the folders and replaced by the most recent form.

BINDERS

Keep the following in binders for handy reference:
Urban Renewal Handbook
Neighborhood Development Program Handbook
HUD circulars, transmittal notices, etc.; index and cross reference
as necessary.
Regional agency letters
Technical guides
Other program handbooks or guides

GENERAL FILES

General files of the LPA should include the following:
1. Workable Program for Community Improvement and related
    data
2. HUD requirements and data concerning Workable Program for
    Community Improvement
3. Related federal and state laws and regulations
4. Data concerning contractors or potential contractors, such as
    planning, title, engineering, land marketing, and appraisal firms
5. Data concerning various HUD programs (i.e., Open Space, Urban
    Beautification, Code Enforcement, Low and Moderate Income
    Housing, etc.)
6. Mortgage financing, including various HUD mortgage insurance
    programs
7. Data regarding other federally related programs, i.e., HEW, VA,
    SBA, etc.
8. Data regarding related state programs
9. Data regarding related professional organizations, including
    NAHRO, American Society of Planning Officials etc.
10. Data concerning local organizations, such as service clubs,
    chambers of commerce, League of Women Voters, etc.
11. Data concerning business and industrial firms, churches, labor
    unions, major property owners, and other individuals and groups
    concerned with community improvement
12. Brochures and data concerning national firms involved in urban
    renewal
13. Data concerning other city, county, and state departments or
    agencies concerned with urban renewal
14. Data and reports from other cities and LPAs

15. Brochures and publications concerning urban renewal and related programs
16. Miscellaneous brochures and catalogues including office supplies and equipment, building materials, etc.
17. Applicable news articles (generally to be pasted on white, uniform sized sheets for easy filing and copying)
18. Obsolete HUD circulars, *Urban Renewal Handbook* pages, etc.
19. Forms (HUD and LPA)

Appendices

Appendices 1, 4, 5
follow herewith.
Appendices 2, 3, 6, 7, 8 and 9 are in a
separate envelope inside the slipcase.

Appendix 1

Suggested Filing System for Urban Renewal
Local Public Agencies

100 ADMINISTRATIVE (LPA)
200 COMMUNITY PLANNING
300 PROJECT MICH. R-47
400 PROJECT MICH. R-84
500 PROJECT MICH. R-102
600 ⎫ Open for future
700 ⎬ urban renewal
800 ⎭ projects
900 GENERAL

100 ADMINISTRATION (LPA)
    110 LPA organization
    113 LPA membership data
    116 LPA by-laws
    119 LPA meetings
    122 Administrative practices
    125 Project applications
        .01 Mich. R-47
            10 Survey and planning
            13 Part I—Loan and grant
            16 Part II—Loan and grant
            19 Amendatory #1
            22 Financial amendatory
        .02 Mich. R-84
        .03 Mich. R-102

128 Contracts
  .01 General
    10 Legal
    13 Administrative consultant
    16 Accounting
    19 Investment
  .03 Project Mich. R-47
    10 Planning advance
    13 Loan and grant
    16 Legal
      -01 Survey and planning
      -03 Execution
      -05 Condemnation
    19 Planning
      -01 Application
      -03 Part I
    21 Title
      -01 Ownership data
      -03 Title insurance
    24 Appraisals
      -01 First acquisition
      -04 Second acquisition
      -07 Fixture
      -10 First reuse
      -13 Second reuse
    27 LUMS or EMAS
    30 Engineering
    33 Demolition
    35 Site clearance and project improvements
  .05 Project Mich. R-84
    Ditto sub-classifications
  .07 Project Mich. R-102
    Ditto sub-classifications
131 Insurance and bonds
  .01 General
    -01 Check signer and co-signer
    -04 Commissioners
    -07 Staff
  .03 Project Mich. R-47
  .05 Project Mich. R-84

.07 Project Mich. R-102
134 Wage rate determinations
    .01 Technical employees
    .04 Laborers and mechanics
137 Budgets
    .01 City
    .04 Approved project budgets and revisions
        -01 Mich. R-47
        -04 Mich. R-84
        -07 Mich. R-102
    .07 Proposed revisions
    .10 Approved annual administrative staff budgets
    .13 Proposed annual administrative staff budgets
    .16 Monthly operating summaries
140 HUD reports (not shown in other files below)
143 Inventory records
146 Personnel records
149 City directives and policies
152 Inter-departmental and inter-agency
155 Director's personal files
158 Audits
    .01 First
    .03 Second
    .05 Consolidated
190 General

200 COMMUNITY PLANNING
    210 Economic resources
        .01 Assessed value
        .04 City finance
        .07 Economic base
        .10 Economic development
        .13 Economic studies
        .16 Employment
        .19 Income
        .22 Labor market
        .25 Taxation
        .90 General
    213 Population
        .01 Attitude survey
        .04 Census material

.07 Community organization
.10 Health and welfare
.13 Old age problems
.16 Population
    -01 Estimates
    -03 Racial
    -05 Vital statistics
.19 Public safety
.22 Techniques
.90 General
216 Geographic
.01 Air pollution
.04 Climate
.07 Flood control
.10 Natural resources
.90 General
219 Design
.01 Aesthetic considerations
.04 Analysis
.07 Concepts
.10 Open space
.13 Site planning
.16 Space needs
.19 Theory
.22 Urban design
.90 General
222 Land use
.01 Commercial
    -01 Central Business District
    -03 Standards
    -05 Signs
.04 Industrial
    -01 Density
    -03 Design
    -05 Location
    -07 Standards
    -09 Proposals
.07 Institutional
    -01 Cemeteries
    -03 Churches
    -05 Miscellaneous

.10 Open and vacant
.13 Residential
    -01 Single family
    -03 Multiple family
    -05 Standards
    -07 Analytical methods
.90 General
225 Transportation—Circulation
  .01 Air transportation
  .04 Expressways
  .07 Parking
  .10 Pedestrian
  .13 Local streets
  .16 Major streets
  .19 Traffic
    -01 Accidents
    -03 Counts
  .22 Transit
  .25 Trucking
  .90 General
228 Community facilities
  .01 Parks and recreation
  .04 Police
  .07 Fire
  .10 Water
  .13 Sewer
  .16 Storm sewer
  .19 Schools
  .22 Libraries
  .25 Civic center
  .28 Hospitals
231 Implementation
  .01 Capital improvements
  .04 Community development
  .07 Continuing planning
    -01 Detailed plans
    -03 Plan adoption
    -05 Plan review
  .10 Development controls
    -01 Building code
    -03 Housing code

    -05 Plumbing code
    -07 Heating code
    -09 Fire prevention code
    -11 Electrical code
    .13 Zoning ordinance
    .15 Subdivision regulations
    .17 Codes and ordinances from other communities
  234 Zoning (active)
  237 Alley vacations (active)
  290 General

300 PROJECT MICH. R-47
  310 Project administration
  313 Project planning
    .01 Eligibility
    .03 Flooding
    .05 Water pollution
    .07 Minority group considerations
    .09 Housing considerations
    .11 Highway programs
    .13 Clearance and redevelopment
    .15 Rehabilitation
    .17 Relocation
    .19 Historic preservation
    .21 Air rights
    .23 Urban renewal plan
    .25 Urban renewal plan changes
    .27 Development plan
    .29 Engineering
    .31 Property acquisition
    .33 Property disposition
    .35 Fiscal data
    .37 Conference reports
    .90 General

300 PROJECT MICH. R-47
  316 Real estate acquisition
    .01 Acquisition appraisals
      -01 First acquisition appraisals
      -04 Second acquisition appraisals
      -07 Fixture appraisals

.03 Requests for HUD concurrence in prices and/or pro-
    claimer documentation

.05 Acquisition authorizations of governing body

.07 List of properties to be acquired

.09 Chronology of acquisition procedures

.50 Acquisition parcel records
       (Maintain a separate file folder for each acquisition
       parcel—file in order of parcel number)

.60 Condemnation record

319 Property management

.01 Tenant files
       (Maintain a separate file folder for each tenant file
       in alphabetical order—same may also be utilized by
       relocation staff)

.03 Tenant ledger

.05 Rent roll

.07 Key files

.09 General correspondence re property management

.11 Contractor's lists

322 Relocation

.01 Relocation surveys

.03 Case files
       (Maintain a separate file folder for each case in alpha-
       betical order based upon current status)

      -01 Occupants at signing of Loan and Grant Contract

      -03 Occupants moving prior to LPA acquiring prop-
          erty

      -05 Temporary on-site moves

      -07 Temporary off-site moves

      -09 Sub-standard relocations—still on work-load

      -11 Sub-standard relocations—removed from work-
          load

      -13 Distant moves—could not inspect

      -15 Relocatee address unknown—still tracing

      -17 Relocatee address unknown—tracing efforts futile

      -19 Satisfactory relocations—still receiving payments

      -21 Satisfactory relocations—removed from work-
          load

.05 Listing files

.07 Relocation payment claims

.09 Determination of average annual gross rentals
.11 Relocation assistance payment records
.13 Small business displacement payment records
.15 Determination of prices—replacement housing
.17 Replacement housing payment records
.19 Relocation reports
.21 Relocation forms, informational statements, guide books, etc.
.23 Control chart
325 Demolition and site clearance
.01 Specifications and contract forms
.03 First invitation of bids
-01 Bid documents and engineers estimate
-03 HUD approval of bid documents
-05 Advertising data
-07 Compilation of bids
-09 Bid documents of unsuccessful bidders
.05 Award of contract—1st invitation
-01 Bid documents and related data of successful bidder
-03 Information concerning sub-contractors
-05 Pre-work conference—equal employment opportunity data
-07 Release orders
-09 Daily inspection and progress reports
-11 Payroll information
-13 Insurance coverages of contractors and subs
-15 Running record of status of each parcel or building
.07 Second invitation of bids
Ditto sub-classifications
.09 Award of contract—2d invitation
Ditto sub-classifications
.50 Force account work
-01 Specifications and plans
-03 Release orders
-05 Progress reports
-07 Payroll records
-09 Basis of city-owned equipment charges
-11 Record of equipment time
-13 Equipment rental costs

-15 Material costs

-17 Running record of status of each parcel or building

.60 Removal of buildings off-site

    -01 List of buildings proposed for removal

    -03 Description of circumstances for removal

    -05 HUD approval

    -07 Advertising data

    -09 Sale data

    -11 Removal and new site data

.70 Removal or relocation of utility lines

    -01 Publicly owned

    -03 Privately owned

    -05 Underground placement

.80 Cross reference site clearance work performed under same contract with project improvement work.

328 Project Improvements

.01 Specifications and contract forms

.03 First invitation of bids

    -01 Bid documents and engineer's estimate

    -03 HUD approval of bid documents

    -05 Advertising data

    -07 Compilation of bids

    -09 Bid documents of unsuccessful bidders

.05 Award of contract—1st invitation

    -01 Bid documents and related data of successful bidder

    -03 Information concerning sub-contractors

    -05 Pre-work conference—equal employment opportunity data

    -07 Release orders

    -09 Daily inspection and progress reports

    -11 Payroll information

    -13 Insurance coverages of contractors and subs

    -15 Change orders

    -17 "As built" drawings

.07 Second invitation of bids

    Ditto sub-classifications

.09 Award of contract—2nd invitation

    Ditto sub-classifications

.50 Force account work

-01 Specifications and plans
-03 HUD concurrence
-05 Release orders
-07 Progress reports
-09 Payroll records
-11 Basis of city-owned equipment charges
-13 Record of equipment time
-15 Equipment rental costs
-17 Material costs
.60 Improvements made by other governmental agencies
.70 Improvements donated by private firms
331 Land marketing and redevelopment
.01 LUMS AND EMAS
.03 Re-use appraisals
.05 Potential developers
.07 First land offering (public)
  -01 Approval of governing body
  -03 Bid documents
  -05 HUD approval of bid documents and/or pro-
      claimer documentation
  -07 Advertising
  -09 Compilation of bids
  -11 Bid award
  -13 HUD mortgage insurance data (residential)
  -15 Unsuccessful bidder data
.09 Second land offering (public)
  Ditto sub-classifications
.25 Negotiated sales
  Maintain a separate file folder for each disposal parcel file in order of parcel number. Include in folder
  the record of negotiations and data of unsuccessful
  developers.
.35 Design competitions
  Maintain a separate file folder for each disposal parcel file in order of parcel number. Include in folder
  all data concerning competition and data concerning
  unsuccessful developers
.50 Disposal parcel records (sales or leases)
  Maintain a separate file folder for each disposal parcel—file in order of parcel number. Include in folder
  the following of successful developer:

a. Bid or negotiation data
b. Offer or bid
c. Non-collusion affidavit
d. Statement of qualifications and financial responsibility.
e. Proposed plans
f. Resolution of award
g. Documentation to HUD
h. HUD approval
i. Public notice (copy)
j. Disposition agreement
k. Development plans
l. Deed, lease or indenture (copy)
m. Certificate of completion (copy)
n. Title commitment and policy (copy)
o. Attorney opinions
.90 Disposal parcel's chronology

334 Rehabilitation
.01 Case file
Maintain a separate file folder for each rehabilitation parcel in order of parcel number. Include all documentation concerning parcel and related rehabilitation activities. Classify as follows:
-01 No rehab. work started
-03 Work in process
-05 Rehab. completed to code
-07 Rehab. completed to PRS
-09 Improvements to property meeting PRS at inception
.03 Inspection records of acquisition properties
.05 Inspection records of properties meeting PRS at inception—no further repairs made
.07 Loans and grants
-01 Pending
-03 Completed
.09 HUD reports
.11 Forms, form letters, etc.
.13 Contractor's listings
.50 Product information

337 Legal
.01 Litigation

.03 Zoning changes
.05 Street and alley vacations
.07 Dedications of land
.09 Replats
.11 Cooperation agreements
.13 Agreements with public utility companies
.15 Easements received, granted, or eliminated
.17 Removal of deed restrictions
.19 Opinions not included under other classifications
340 Project financing
   .01 Planning advances
        -01 First requisition for planning advance
        -03 Second requisition for planning advance
   .03 Note resolutions
   .05 Direct federal loans
        -01 First requisition and related documents
        -03 Second requisition and related documents
   .07 Federally secured private financing
        -01 First loan and related documents
        -03 Second loan and related documents
   .09 Local financing
   .11 Investment of excess cash
        -01 Bank agreement and related documents
        -03 Record of investments
   .13 Transfers of project funds
        -01 HUD approvals
        -03 Record of transfers
   .15 Local cash grants-in-aid
        -01 Data concerning first grant
        -03 Data concerning second grant
   .17 Local non-cash grants-in-aid—by locality
        -01 Data concerning land donations
        -03 Data concerning first non-cash grant
        -05 Data concerning second non-cash grant
   .19 Local non-cash grants-in-aid—schools
   .21 Local non-cash grants-in-aid—public housing
   .23 Local non-cash grants-in-aid—colleges and universities
   .25 Local non-cash grants-in-aid—hospitals
   .27 Local non-cash grants-in-aid—county
   .29 Local non-cash grants-in-aid—state
   .31 Local non-cash grants-in-aid—private firms

343 Accounting
 .01 Copies of contracts
 .03 Pending purchase orders
 .05 Completed purchase orders and related data
 .07 Unpaid invoices
 .09 Paid invoices and related data
 .11 Payroll records
  -01 Time and attendance records
  -03 Leave records
  -05 Breakdown of time (if applicable)
  -07 Payroll withholdings
  -09 Withholding tax reports
 .13 Travel expense vouchers
 .15 Copies bank deposit slips
 .17 Petty cash vouchers
 .19 Copies of check vouchers
 .21 Bank statements and reconciliation
 .23 Copies form HUD-6250 (Report of budgetary status)
 .25 Copies monthly operating summary
 .27 Copies form HUD-6251 (Project balance sheet)
 .29 Data concerning investments
346 Citizen participation
 .01 Project area committee
  -01 Membership list
  -03 Meeting minutes
  -05 Record of conferences
  -07 Committee studies, reports, and recommenda-
    tions
  -09 Plans and proposals of technical advisors
 .03 Other citizen organization activities
 .05 Participation of individuals and business firms
 .07 News media
 .09 Other citizen participation

900 GENERAL
 910 Workable program (local)
 913 HUD Workable program data
 916 Laws and regulations
  .01 Federal
  .03 State
  .05 Local
 919 Data concerning contractors and potential contractors

.01 Planning
.03 Title
.05 Engineering
.07 Land marketing
.09 Appraising
922 HUD programs
.01 Open space
.03 Urban beautification
.05 Code enforcement
.07 Demolition grant
.09 Low income housing
.11 Rent supplement
925 Mortgage financing
.01 FHA
.03 Conventional
928 Related federal programs
.01 HEW
.03 VA
.05 SBA
.07 Office of Economic Opportunity
931 Related state programs
934 Related county programs
937 Other public programs
.01 Drainage district
.03 Council of governments
.05 Sanitary district
937 Professional organizations
.01 American Society of Planning Officials
.03 International City Management Association
.05 NAHRO
.07 National Housing Conference
940 Local organizations
.01 Chamber of Commerce
.03 Exchange Club
.05 Kiwanis
.07 League of Women Voters
.09 Rotary
943 Business and industrial firms (local)
946 Labor organizations
949 National firms

952 Data from other cities and LPAs
955 Brochures and data concerning urban renewal
958 Miscellaneous brochures and catalogues
    .01 Building material and supplies
    .03 Office supplies and equipment
961 News articles
964 Obsolete regulations and directives
    .01 HUD circulars and transmittal notices
    .03 *Urban Renewal Handbook* pages
990 Forms
    Maintain a separate file folder for each form number
    —File in numerical order.
    .01 HUD forms
    .03 LPA forms
    .05 Sample forms from other agencies

Appendix 4

Form No. (R) 300-11

Informational Statement
(Residential)

Lincoln Park Department of Urban Renewal
1355 Southfield Road
Lincoln Park, Michigan

THIS IS VERY IMPORTANT   READ IT

The building in which you live has been purchased by the City of Lincoln Park Urban Renewal Department. This and other buildings within the project area will be torn down and the land resold for various new purposes. In order that the redevelopment of the land may proceed without delay, it is necessary that you find another place in which to live; however, pending the relocation of your family, you may continue to use and occupy the premises commonly known as ....
.... with the following understanding:

Only persons now in occupancy are to be permitted to remain in occupancy and should any of them move elsewhere, the rooms they occupied shall not be re-let without our consent.

No part of the premises is to be used for illegal or immoral purposes.

Representatives of the Lincoln Park Urban Renewal Department are to be permitted access to your unit at all reasonable hours.

140

Your starting date of tenancy is the .... day of ....,
19.....
Your rent will be due on the .... day of ....,
19.....
Rent to be charged will be $............ per month, payable in
advance on or before the .... day of each month at the Treasurer's
Office, or the Urban Renewal Office, City of Lincoln Park, 1355
Southfield Road, Lincoln Park, Michigan.
Rent paid in advance will be refunded on a pro-rata basis to the
date that you move.
All utilities are to be paid by you except ....
....

The foregoing is offered you with the clear understanding that it is
for the sole purpose of allowing you temporary use of the premises until you vacate. Accordingly, your tenancy will be on a monthly basis
with the right of termination in either party upon service of written
notice. The Urban Renewal Department requests your cooperation in
carrying out its responsibility under the law to manage its buildings
properly and to relocate families displaced. The Urban Renewal Department is empowered to carry out eviction for any of the following
reasons:

1. Failure to pay rent
2. Maintenance of a nuisance or use of premises for illegal purposes
3. Material breach of the Terms of Occupancy
4. Refusal to admit Urban Renewal representatives
5. Refusal to consider adequate relocation housing

The Department of Urban Renewal will help you find another place
to live. The law requires that any place the Department finds for you
must be "decent, safe and sanitary." Until you find a good, sound, safe
place in which to live or until the Department finds the same you will
not be required to move. However, you may be required to move on a
temporary basis if the progress schedule of the project requires the
demolition of your dwelling.
In our office located at 1355 Southfield Road (2nd floor), our Relocation Staff will be available to help you. The office is open from 9:00
a.m. to 5:00 p.m. Monday through Friday, and 6:00 to 8:00 Monday
evenings. The Relocation staff will keep in touch with you through
visits to your home and seeing you in the office in order to give you

every assistance in finding good housing. We will have lists of standard houses for rent and for sale. These lists are available to you.

Please start now to look for a place to live that meets good housing standards. If you find your own place, notify the Relocation Office at once.

The Department of Urban Renewal will help you move by paying actual charges by a licensed mover not to exceed $200. or if you wish to move yourself, we would pay on a per room basis as outlined on page 9 of your "Facts on Relocation" booklet.

If you prefer to have your actual moving expenses paid you must notify the Relocation Officer at least one week prior to move. The Department will then advise you and the moving firm by mail that the proposed moving arrangements were approved. In such case, the Department will pay the mover directly.

Certain property owners and tenants may be entitled to additional relocation payments. These are explained in your "Facts on Relocation" booklet, and if you are eligible, our Relocation staff will explain these benefits in greater detail.

It is necessary to notify the Office of the Department of Urban Renewal prior to moving. Failure to do so may affect your relocation benefits.

Yours truly,
CITY OF LINCOLN PARK
DEPARTMENT OF URBAN RENEWAL
by Emanuel Gorland
Director

The above informational statement has been read and explained to me. I understand my obligations and the assistance I will receive from the Department of Urban Renewal.

I have received my "Facts on Relocation" booklet.

I also understand that as long as I live at the above address, I am to pay $ . . . . rent each month in advance at either the Treasurer's Office or the Urban Renewal Office, 1355 Southfield Road, and that the first payment is due on the . . . . day of . . . ., 19 . . . . .

Date . . . .   Signed . . . .

TABULATION OF REAL ESTATE TAX PAYMENTS

YEAR ....

TAX RATE ....

PARCEL NO.	LEGAL DE-SCRIPTION	DATES		ASSESSED VALUATION			TAXES			
		ACQUI-SITION	DISPO-SITION[1]	LAND	IMPROVE-MENTS	TOTAL	TOTAL[2]	AMOUNT PRO-RATED TO ORIG-INAL OWNER	AMOUNT PRO-RATED TO DEVELOPER	ELIGIBLE LPA TAX[3]

[1] If disposed during tax year.

[2] Total assessed valuation X tax rate.

[3] Amount prorated to original owner plus amount prorated to developer (if disposed during same tax year) subtracted from total taxes paid during tax year.

NOTE:

If tax levy dates differ for jurisdiction i.e. county, city, school district, separate calculations should be made for each such jurisdiction. They are then added together to obtain the total tax payment and tax credit.

143

TABULATION OF REAL ESTATE TAX CREDITS

YEAR ....

TAX RATE ....

PARCEL NO.	LEGAL DESCRIPTION	DATES			ASSESSED VALUATION[1]			NO. OF MONTHS CREDIT ALLOWABLE[2]	AMOUNT OF ALLOWABLE CREDIT[3]
		ACQUI-SITION	DEMO-LITION	DISPO-SITION	LAND	IMPROVE-MENTS	TOTAL		

[1] Last established prior to acquisition.

[2] Twelve months unless disposed during year, if disposed prorate to month of disposition.

[3] To determine multiply total assessed valuation by tax rate X number of months credit allowable.

$\frac{}{12}$

NOTE:

If tax levy dates differ for jurisdiction i.e. county, city, school district, separate calculations should be made for each such jurisdiction. They are then added together to obtain the total tax payment and tax credit.

Abbreviations

CRP Community Renewal Program
EMAS Economic and Market Analysis Study
GNRA General Neighborhood Renewal Area
GNRP General Neighborhood Renewal Program
HEW U. S. Department of Health, Education and Welfare
HUD U. S. Department of Housing and Urban Development
LPA Local Public Agency
LUMS Land Utilization and Marketability Study
NAHRO National Association of Housing and Redevelopment
      Officials
NDP Neighborhood Development Program
PAC Project Area Committee
PRS Property Rehabilitation Standards
SBA Small Business Administration
VA Veterans' Administration

The author, Emanuel Gorland, received his J.D. degree from Brooklyn Law School and his M.P.A. degree from New York University. He supervises urban renewal, low rent housing, and other community improvement programs as director of community improvement, Lincoln Park, Michigan.

The manuscript was edited by Marguerite C. Wallace. The book and jacket were designed by Joanne Colman. The text type used is Caledonia designed by W. A. Dwiggins in 1937, and the display type is Univers designed by Adrian Frutiger in 1960.

The text is printed on Bradford Book paper. The book is bound in Columbia Mills' Fictionette Natural Finish cloth over binders' boards. Manufactured in the United States of America.